Charles Montesquieu

The temple of Gnidus

With the original copper-plate engravings from the design of C. Eisen and Le

Barbier

Charles Montesquieu

The temple of Gnidus
With the original copper-plate engravings from the design of C. Eisen and Le Barbier

ISBN/EAN: 9783337197667

Hergestellt in Europa, USA, Kanada, Australien, Japan

Cover: Foto ©Andreas Hilbeck / pixelio.de

Weitere Bücher finden Sie auf **www.hansebooks.com**

THE
TEMPLE
OF GNIDUS

By

Charles de Secondat
BARON DE MONTESQUIEU

.... non murmura vestra Columbæ,
Brachia non Hederæ, non vincant oscula Conchæ.

LONDON:
VIZETELLY & CO.
Henrietta Street.
Covent Garden.

THE

TEMPLE OF GNIDUS;

FOLLOWED BY

CEPHISA AND CUPID, AND ARSACES AND ISMENIA.

BY

C. DE SECONDAT, BARON DE MONTESQUIEU,

WITH A PREFACE BY OCTAVE UZANNE.

ILLUSTRATED WITH THE ORIGINAL COPPER-PLATE ENGRAVINGS
FROM THE DESIGNS OF C. EISEN AND LE BARBIER.

Lemaire inv   Depollier sc

LONDON:

VIZETELLY & CO., 16, *HENRIETTA STREET*,

COVENT GARDEN.

CONTENTS

CONTENTS.

—◦◦⟩◦⟨◦◦—

LIST OF PLATES.

———◦◦∘∻∘◦◦———

LETTER TO A LADY BY WAY OF PREFACE.

"O Venus Regina Gnidi Paphique!"—*Horace*

HE author of *The Persian Letters*, that passionate lover of antiquity, was we are assured, ever ready to say like Pliny: "it is to Athens that you are bound; respect the gods." To-day, Madam, we are about to repair to Gnidus, to a pretty temple of pink marble, with a rococo pediment covered with cupids—not a Parthenon corresponding with a temple of the Virgin, but an edifice of less haughty majesty and more entrancing aspect. And there is no need for me to parody Pliny and Montesquieu and murmur in your ear, "Respect the goddess," for I am aware that you are fully disposed to revere a divinity to whom your beauty renders perpetual homage.

B

Picture the departure for Cythera, in a world where
everything is exquisitely conventional.   Here dancing
upon the crystal waters appear the nacreous shells of
Venus, which her white doves will presently conduct.
The balmy and breezeless atmosphere is charged with
subtle perfumes.   With delicious harmony the nymphs
and dryads mingle their voices in the depths of the woods,
and far away in the blurred distance—the bluey land of
dreams—one can espy the coquettish little altar, lighted
by a soft ruby tinted sun, whither we are about to repair
on pilgrimage.

Quickly don that Watteau costume which becomes you
so well, and those vair-trimmed shoes worthy of Cinderella.
Skilfully place a few patches on your cheeks to ensure a
languid glance or an ironical smile.   Scatter a cloudlet of
powder in your hair, that your black velvetty eyes may
acquire a more voluptuous expression beneath the snowy
hoar—so truly charming.   Take, I pray you, that fantas-
tical Chinese fan, and let us start.

What ! you have not read the little Greek book I sent
you ?   "What times are ours," said the author, "when
there are so many judges and critics and so few readers ? "
Still, I will not scold you too severely for not having filled
up this blank in your stock of erudition—indeed, how
could I do so since to your charming negligence I owe the
great happiness of serving as your guide to the book, the
perusal of which you are about to begin—like the pretty
delicate *gourmet* you are, with a taste for delightful trifles.

I suspect that, like myself, you already know the
celebrated President de Montesquieu by his works, *The
Spirit of the Laws, The Essay upon Taste,* and the *Familiar
Letters;* however that may be, I cannot refrain from

placing before you this malicious literary pastel, forming part of the portrait-gallery of that querulous but witty monkey, the little Abbé de Voisenon :—

" Montesquieu is one of the men who have conferred the most honour upon France. He is not like those authors who incessantly revolve in the same circle and spend their lives in re-writing the same one book under twenty different titles. *The Temple of Gnidus, The Persian Letters, The Decline of the Romans,* and the *Spirit of the Laws* are all four of very different styles. The author appears in turn as the painter of the Graces, as a shrewd and amusing censor, as a philosophical historian, and as a learned legislator. He was elected a member of the French Academy for having written *The Persian Letters,* but on the condition that he would disavow them; and *The Temple of Gnidus* procured him the favours of beauty upon condition that he should keep his good fortune a secret. He was very fond of women, and extremely well acquainted with men, whom he consequently held in scant esteem. However, as he was not unsociable, he consorted with them, being indeed of the opinion that we need the society of our fellow creatures. He was so fond a father that in all good faith he believed his son to be superior to himself. He was an affectionate and firm friend. His converse was diversified like his writings. He was gay and thoughtful in turn, an adept in argument, and at the same time a ready narrator. He was also extremely absent-minded. He started one day from Fontainebleau and sent his carriage on before him, purposing to follow it upon foot for an hour or so, in view of taking exercise. He thus went as far as Villejuif, fancying that he had gone no farther than Chailly. His book, the

Spirit of the Laws, has been translated into every language and will become a classical work in every country, despite the clamour of devotees and the criticisms of the Sorbonne, of Fréron, and even of M. Dupin. The *Gazette Ecclésiastique* considered it necessary to censure this work severely out of Christian charity; whereupon the President de Montesquieu made so bold as to reply by an apology which is a model of eloquence and delicate wit. When the Jansenist writer of the criticism in the *Gazette* found himself thus confounded, he declared that the President was an Atheist. M. de Montesquieu died, however, professing Christian sentiments, and saying that the morality of the New Testament was excellent and the finest gift that God could have made to man! In spite of this, those who are expert in such matters assert that he is damned."

Is not the Abbé's pen and ink sketch delicately executed? One may especially commend the final shaft—" Those who are expert in such matters assert that he is damned." Voisenon himself—" that little handful of fleas," as the Marquis de Polignac called him—was very expert in regard to damnation. Did he not carry his dissolute behaviour into the hermitage of the Favarts, and the fiend alone knows how shrewd and cunning he then proved. But I must call your attention to a remark which I am bound to explain to you :—" *The Temple of Gnidus*," says Voisenon, " procured him the favours of beauty upon the condition that he should keep his good fortune a secret." This is, indeed, one of those bitterly ironical remarks—an example of the *nescio quid acetum*, which is to be found throughout the writings of the author of *Sultan Misapouf*. It leads me to relate to you without further preamble the origin of this pretty *Temple of Gnidus,* which you are about to peruse so devoutly.

Montesquieu, who penned the charming *mot :* "I am in love with friendship," was also the friend, indeed, the great friend, of love, and I can easily support this statement by quoting to you these various avowals which he has made in his works : "In my youth," he says, "I was sufficiently fortunate to attach myself to women who, to my belief, loved me ; as soon as I ceased to believe this I abruptly drew away from them." Farther on he writes : "I have been rather fond of saying soft things to women, and of rendering them those services which cost one so little." Again : "At the age of five-and-thirty I was still in love." Couple the foregoing declarations with this one : "I have been so foolish as to write books and to feel ashamed of them when I had written them "—and then you will in some wise have the synthesis of *The Temple of Gnidus.*

I will not assert with serene assurance like Voisenon that this pretty poem in prose procured its author the favours of women ; I rather incline to the belief that it was a piece of good fortune of the kind that induced the President to erect this dainty little temple as an *ex voto* to the divinity of Paphos.

Montesquieu was over four-and-thirty when he penned this Grecian booklet, which appears to have had a key, nowadays as difficult to find intact as that of *The Dangerous Connections,* lost no one knows where ; and this key would appear to have been formed of the following alloyage :—

"Président-à-Mortier" of the Bordeaux Parliament since the year 1716, already renowned for his wit and literary talents, Montesquieu towards 1723 was made welcome and much of both in Paris and at Court. He also had free access to Chantilly, and those were the palmy days of Chantilly, which the *précieuses* of the previous century had named Cyprus, at the period when the Duchess de Longueville was sighing in the arbours of Sylvia. But in Montesquieu's time there was less *préciosité* and more gallantry in this princely abode. Here the Marchioness de Prie reigned, and in the brilliant dissolute little Court around her a prominent place was held by Mademoiselle de Clermont, sister of the Duke de Bourbon, who became Minister to Louis XV. upon the death of the Regent.

I might here weave a romance or some kind of fairy tale to interest you; but this would be treating you like a child, or turning you into a dupe ; so I will content myself with simply chronicling the facts to allay your impatience, and keep this epistle within bounds.

Mademoiselle de Clermont was about twenty-seven years of age at the time I speak of. Natier painted her at this period in all her nymph-like freshness, amid an allegorical scene in which Youth and Love were shown attentive to her service. Nothing can be more graceful and more provoking than her voluptuous face as it appears amid these surroundings borrowed from Grecian mythology. You are no doubt acquainted with this curious painting which has often been engraved ; it is perfect, and would have furnished a fitting frontispiece for *The Temple of Gnidus*, since she whom it represents inspired that dainty masterpiece.

Mademoiselle de Clermont was not, however, one of those ideal vestals who kindle fires but to fan the flames, and never extinguish them. The example set her by her two brothers, the Duke de Bourbon and the Count de Clermont was in no wise calculated to ensure the practice of virtue. A friend of Madame de Prie, the wittiest but also the most cunning and most perverted of marchionesses, participating in every diversion, joining in the hunting parties during the day-time, and in the little orgies at night, elbowing the damsels of the opera, and listening to scandalous tales and anecdotes, Mademoiselle de Clermont had already tripped upon one occasion, falling into the arms of the Duke de Melun, who had subsequently died from an accident in the hunting field—July, 1722. This adventure alone would be of small importance, but the author of a *Histoire de Montesquieu* adds: " She ate a great deal, she drank more than was good for her, and she composed songs of so filthy a character that the king called her ' The Muse of the Dunghill ! ' "

This is horrible; and it must be supposed that this dragon of vice could, when she chose, exercise great powers of fascination, since Montesquieu succumbed to her like the Duke de Melun had done. History has chronicled the fact that he was wont to kiss Mademoiselle de Clermont on the lips, and the rough drafts of three of his letters, published in recent times,[1] show us that there was a thorough intrigue between them. The first of these letters is a declaration in passionate language; another alludes to a *tête-à-tête* which was unfortunately interrupted by the arrival of a visitor; and the third, which is of a fragmentary character, runs as follows :—

" Your haughtiness does not intimidate me. Why should I not live under the sway of her whom I love? I will comply with your orders in every respect. I am

---

[1] *Histoire de Montesquieu*, by Louis Vian, Paris, 1875, pp. 76-77.

sorry that your people do not start for Versailles and that I am condemned to live so near to you without seeing you. You wholly occupy my thoughts, you are both the worry of my mind and the delight of my heart.

" Farewell, Madam, I should be happy if to-night—but it is of no avail for me to speak of my desires and my regret."

Believe me, my dear Madam, Montesquieu's desires were ultimately satisfied, and if he afterwards retained any regret it was the regret one feels in stirring up the embers of a passion that has been requited but is so no longer. However, let us return to the little temple of which I have promised you the history, to the work which Madame du Deffant, imitating D'Alembert, called " The Apocalypse of Gallantry."

The Count de Clermont and the Marchioness de Prie took part in a burlesque mythological *fête* given at the Château of Bellébat in 1724. Voltaire, who contributed some verses on this occasion—verses set to music by the village priest of Courdemanche, " whose head was full of rhymes and melodies "—afterwards penned a narrative of this *fête*, couched in very obscene language, and boldly offered a copy of his work to Mademoiselle de Clermont. It was then that Montesquieu, in his indignation, erected *The Temple of Gnidus* to show the cynical Voltaire how an amorous subject should be treated, without offending against the laws of decency. *The Fête of Bellébat* had been sent to the Duke de Bourbon's sister ; and it was for her alone that the President composed this voluptuous prose poem of the *Temple*, the various scenes of which resemble so many paintings by Boucher and Lancret, executed with that delicacy of touch and displaying that freshness of colouring peculiar to the so-called "*peintres des fêtes galantes.*"

This poem—between the lines of which one could easily read at the time of its publication—literally teems with allusions. Gnidus is Chantilly with its palace, its shady underwoods, its groves, its fountains, its cosy little corners where merry beauties disported themselves at blind man's buff, at hide-and-seek, at swinging to and fro—when not engaged in more naughty and dangerous pastimes. "There," says the writer, "the sacrifices are sighs and the offerings are tender hearts. Each lover addresses his vows to his mistress, and Venus receives them for her."

In the goddess one seems to recognise the proud Marchioness de Prie—

> Cet esprit juste, gracieux,
> Solide dans le sérieux
> Et charmant dans les bagatelles—

that haughty favourite who would not survive her disgrace but died of despair, like a Cleopatra of the Regency, in the bitterness of exile. The name of Themira is but a transparent muslin mask set before Mademoiselle de Clermont's face; and Montesquieu was intimately acquainted with the prototype of Aristæus (President Hénault, so it is said), and indeed with the originals of all the characters whom he brings upon the scene. I will add nothing further else I might rob you of the pleasure which one derives from the unexpected ; and besides to my mind, nothing can be more agreeable than to muse in uncertainty upon the allusions of such a book as this. Your imagination has already fled to the land of dreams and I abandon it to its resources. It is more competent than all the Cuviers of history to unravel the details of this narrative of a passion long dead and buried.

c

But lo! here steps in the tiresome bibliographer, the historian of books, learned in the genealogies of multitudinous editions. Pray do not pout. I will exert myself to make the lesson as short and as free from pedantry as possible. I have no intention of emptying into your brain a whole cartload of editions of every size and style, or of compiling a list of the many piracies, squibs, and repetitions to which Montesquieu's little book gave rise. No, I will simply tell you what it is fitting you should not remain ignorant of. There shall be no learned symphony, merely a modest little overture before the rise of the curtain.

The Temple of Gnidus was not intended for the press. It was but an argument *ad mulierem*, and Montesquieu, in penning it, displayed rather a lover's vanity than an author's care. But curiosity pokes its nose everywhere, exerting itself in proportion to the amount of mystery and intrigue that it desires to unravel. Scarcely had Mademoiselle de Clermont received the manuscript of her admirer than numerous copies of it began to circulate in society, and in September, 1724, a publication called *La Bibliothèque Française*, appearing at Amsterdam, published the full text, just referring to the author in the following paragraph : " This composition has been too well received by the public not to be included among those fugitive writings which are worthy of being preserved. We are assured that the style is that of the author who gave us *The Persian Letters*."

The first separate edition of *The Temple of Gnidus* appeared anonymously in Paris in the early part of the following year. It was issued by Nicholas Simart, bookseller, and comprised eighty-two pages, 12mo. Besides writing a preface, which you will find further on, Montesquieu had slightly revised the text for this edition. It was just referred to by Matthieu Marais who wrote as follows in his *Journal,* under date April 10, 1725: " *The Temple of Gnidus,* a little semi-Grecian book, the allusions of which are full of transparent obscenity. It is printed with the King's approbation and privilege. It appeared during Holy Week and caused a scandal. It is attributed to President de Montesquieu of Bordeaux, author of *The Persian Letters.*"

It was very absurd and audacious on Marais' part to talk of the obscenity of a work in which the Graces alone reign supreme. Still the President would not acknowledge himself to be the architect of the little *Temple,* declaring that his time was otherwise employed, either in attending to his judicial functions or in writing serious works. Indeed, he had long been engaged upon his *Spirit of the Laws,* and was upon the point of publishing his *Considerations upon the Greatness and Decline of the Romans.* " With reference to the works that are attributed to me," he wrote to his friend Moncrif, " I am situated like La Fontaine-Martel was in regard to the ridiculous characteristics imputed to him. They are ascribed to me but I deny them." The deceitful fellow ! That monster, the Marquis de Sade, never more flatly denied the paternity of *Justine*.

Meanwhile *The Temple of Gnidus* went through numerous editions and appeared at Paris, London, and Leyden with Montesquieu's name upon the title-page. The father, who, for fear of compromising himself, shrinks from acknowledging his illegitimate offspring, is exposed to see his child boldly assume his name upon attaining his majority. As it is in human life so it is with books. The

President at last acknowledged himself conquered and even revised his preface, inserting in it the following tender declaration: " With regard to the fair sex to whom I am indebted for the few happy moments I have known in life, I trust with all my heart that this work will please it. I still adore the sex, and though it is no longer the object of my occupations it is that of my regrets."

To complete these remarks I must quote the following passage concerning *The Temple of Gnidus* from D'Alembert's *Elogium of Montesquieu*. The great admirer of Mademoiselle de Lespinasse shows himself favourable to the tender lover of Mademoiselle de Clermont: " *The Temple of Gnidus*," he says, "followed soon after *The Persian Letters*. In the latter, Montesquieu had figured as Horace, Theophrastes, and Lucian, in this new effort he appeared as Ovid and Anacreon. He no longer purposed depicting the despotic love of the East but the delicacy and *naïveté* of pastoral love, such as may exist in a heart which has not yet been corrupted by intercourse with mankind. Fearing, perhaps, that a picture of something so foreign to our customs might appear tame and monotonous the author has endeavoured to improve it by giving it a gay and animated setting. He conducts the reader to enchanted spots, which although they may be of little interest to the ardent lover are of a nature to flatter the imagination when the desires are satisfied. Carried away by his subject, the writer has employed that animated, figurative, poetical style, of which the romance of *Telemachus* furnished us with the first pattern. We do not know why certain censors of *The Temple of Gnidus* should have asserted that it needed to be written in verse. Poetical style, if by this term one understands—as should be the case—a style full of warmth and imagery, does not need the uniform cadence of versification to prove agreeable; but if one merely understands by poetical style an abundance of useless epithets, cold, trivial descriptions of Cupid's wings and bow, versification, however rhythmical, will not impart any merit to such writing as this. Life and soul will ever be wanting in it. But whatever be the case in that respect, *The Temple of Gnidus* being a species of poem in prose, it is for our most celebrated writers in that department to decide what rank it should occupy: it is deserving of such judges; and for our own part we believe that the pictures of this work would successfully sustain one of the greatest tests that can be applied to poetical descriptions—that of being conveyed to canvas. Moreover, what should be more especially remarked in *The Temple of Gnidus* is that Anacreon here shows himself both an observer and a philosopher."

The fact that the book was "a poem in prose" became a positive charge against Montesquieu, whom Voltaire, author of *The Temple of Taste*, accused of treason against poetry. But this was trivial criticism. Montesquieu did right to avoid the shoals and breakers which only presumptuous mediocrity dares to brave. It was he himself who wrote: "Poets are authors who make it their business to fetter common sense and who bury reason beneath ornaments, just as women were formerly entombed in a mass of finery and jewels." And indeed, if in that time of poetical insipidity anyone was more guilty than others of treason, it was not Montesquieu, but Colardeau who was destined to avenge him upon Voltaire.

I am not quite sure whether some madman did not

disguise Fenelon's *Telemachus* in alexandrines, but at all events I know right well that Colardeau, the author of *The Trickery in Fashion,* covered himself with ridicule by arraying the *Temple of Gnidus* in a carnival dress of paltry verses, worthy at the utmost of being cut up for insertion in the " demon-crackers " and other sweetmeats of the eighteenth century.

I shall not speak to you of the edition you are about to examine—a counterpart of one of the most wonderful volumes of the last century—one of the rare works only found in the cabinets of wealthy bibliophilists. I perceive that I have neglected to tell you many things in the course of this hastily written letter, but I know that you willingly forgive the absent-minded, and besides I agree with the Prince de Ligne in thinking that women are too witty already and need the curb. So I will stop here, the better to restrain you—the shortest lessons are said to be the best. Now turn the page, for Montesquieu is awaiting you to do you the honours of his Temple.—Farewell, Themira, we must part !

OCTAVE UZANNE.

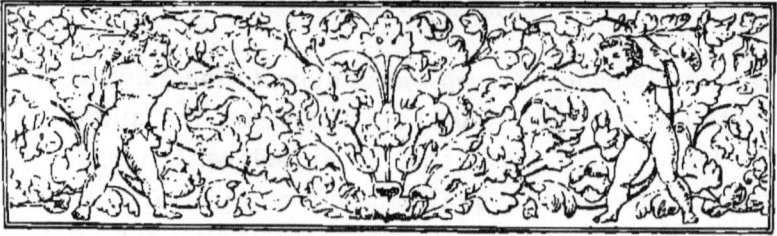

TRANSLATOR'S PREFACE.*

A FRENCH ambassador at the Sublime Porte, well-known by his taste for letters, purchased several Greek manuscripts and took them with him to France. Some of these manuscripts having fallen into my hands, I found among them the work of which I here offer a translation.

Few Greek poets have reached us. Many of them perished in the destruction of the libraries, or through the negligence of the families which possessed them.

From time to time we recover some fragments of these treasures. Certain writings have even been found in the tombs of their authors; and, what amounts to the same, this work was found among the books of a Greek bishop.

* This is Montesquieu's original preface, he desiring it to be supposed that the work was simply a translation from the Greek.

This poem does not resemble any work of the kind that we possess, though the rules which the poetical authors found in nature are observed.

The description of Gnidus contained in the first Canto is the more felicitous as it, so to say, gives birth to the poem. It is not an adornment of the subject, but part of the subject itself, thus being very different from those foreign and far-fetched descriptions which the Ancients so strongly blamed :—

> Purpureus latè qui splendeat, unus et alter
> Assuitur pannus.

The episodes of the second and third Cantos are also the outcome of the subject, and the poet has proceeded with so much art that the ornaments of his poem are also necessary parts thereof.

There is as much art in the fourth and fifth Cantos. The poet having to show Aristæus narrating his amours with Camilla does not allow the son of Autilochus to recount his adventures farther than his meeting with Themira, his object being to impart some variety to the narratives.

The story of Aristæus and Camilla is uncommon inasmuch as it is purely a story of sentiments.

The crisis occurs in the sixth Canto, and the close is very ably brought about in the seventh by a mere glance from Themira.

The poet does not enter into details upon the reconciliation of Aristæus and Camilla. He just mentions it, that the reader may know it has taken place, but he adds nothing further, wishing to avoid a defective uniformity.

The purpose of the poem is to show that we owe our happiness to the sentiments of the heart, and not to the pleasures of the senses, and that no bliss is ever so complete that it may not be disturbed by misadventures.

It should be remarked that the Cantos are not separated from one another in the Greek manuscript, which is very ancient. There is merely a note upon the margin at the beginning of each of them.

Neither the name of the author nor the period at which he lived is known. All that one can say on this point is, that he was not prior to Sappho, since he mentions her in his work. There is reason, however, to believe that he lived prior to Terence, and that the latter has imitated a passage at the close of the second Canto; for there is no proof that our author was a plagiarist, whereas Terence stole from the Greeks, to such an extent indeed, that in one of his comedies he combined two plays by Menander.

I at first had the design of publishing the original side by side with the translation; but I have been advised to issue the Greek text in a separate edition with the learned notes, which an erudite scholar is preparing, and which will soon be ready for the light.

As for my translation, it is a faithful one. I considered

that such beauties as I did not find in my author were not beauties, and I selected the expressions which seemed to me to render his meaning most closely, even when these expressions were not of the best.

I was encouraged to make this translation by the success which has attended that of Tasso. He who made the latter will not take it amiss if I venture upon the same course as himself. He has distinguished himself in such a manner that he has nothing whatever to fear, even from those whom he has invested with the greatest spirit of emulation.

THE TEMPLE OF GNIDUS.

CANTO I.

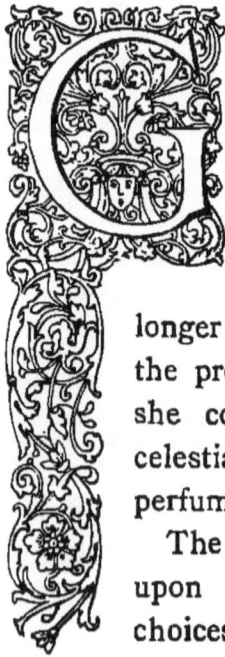

GNIDUS is the favourite abode of Venus; she prefers it to that of Paphos, or of Amathonta. She never descends from Olympus without visiting the Gnidians; and she has so much accustomed that happy people to behold her, that they are no longer affected with the sacred horror which the presence of a deity inspires. Sometimes she conceals herself in a cloud, but the celestial odour which exhales from her locks, perfumed with ambrosia, betrays the goddess.

The city stands in the midst of a country upon which heaven has poured forth its choicest blessings with a liberal hand: here reign the glories of eternal spring; the bountiful earth anticipates every wish; innumerable flocks feed on the plains; the winds breathe only to convey the perfume of the flowers; the birds sing with unceasing melody; you would think that the woods were vocal; the rivulets murmur through the valleys; a genial warmth makes everything teem with life; and pleasure is inhaled with every breeze.

Near the city stands the palace of Venus. Vulcan himself laid its foundations, and reared it for his false spouse, when he wished to make her forget the cruel affront that he had offered her in the presence of all the gods.

It is impossible for a mortal to describe the beauties of this palace: the Graces alone are equal to the task. Gold and azure, and rubies and diamonds shine in every corner—but I am painting its riches, not its beauties.

The gardens seem the work of enchantment: Flora and Pomona have made them their peculiar care, and they are cultivated by the nymphs of these goddesses: the fruits grow under the hand that gather them, and flowers succeed the fruits. When Venus walks in these enchanted gardens, surrounded by her fair votaries, the young Gnidian women, you would think that, in their wanton sports, the delicate beauties of the delightful place would be entirely destroyed; but, by some secret power, every injury is repaired in a moment.

Venus takes pleasure in beholding the artless dances of the daughters of Gnidus; her nymphs mingle among them; the goddess herself takes part in their sports;

she lays aside the majesty of her divinity, seats herself in the midst of them, and views with delight the joy and innocence that reign in their hearts.

A spacious meadow is discovered at a distance, quite enamelled with flowers; these the shepherd comes to gather with his fair shepherdess; but the flower that she gathers is always the most beautiful, and he fancies that Flora has made it on purpose for her.

The river Cepheus waters this meadow, through which he makes a thousand meanders. He stays the flying shepherdesses, and forces them to give the tender kiss they have promised him.

When the nymphs approach his banks, he stops; he smooths the undulation of his waters: but when any one of them bathes, he becomes still more amorous, and his waves surround her; sometimes he swells that he may the more perfectly embrace her; he lifts her up, he flies, he bears her away. Her alarmed companions begin to weep; but he supports her upon his bosom; and charmed with so precious a burden, he carries her over his liquid plain, till at last, with sorrow at being obliged to quit her, he sets her down in safety on the shore, and relieves the anxiety of her weeping companions.

Near this meadow there is a myrtle wood with a thousand winding pathways. Hither come the love-sick swains and the amorous shepherdesses, to relate the story of their pleasing pains. Love, who consoles them, leads them through paths that become more and more retired.

At no great distance there is an ancient and sacred

forest, into which the light of day can hardly penetrate. Oaks, that look as if they were immortal, hide their heads in the clouds. Here a religious awe takes possession of the mind. You would think this spot had been the dwelling-place of the gods before men came forth from the bosom of the earth.

Upon issuing from the solemn obscurity of the wood, a little hill presents itself, on which stands the temple of Venus. The universe has nothing more sacred, nothing more venerable than this place.

It was in this temple that the young Adonis first appeared before Venus. The sweet poison instantly darted into the heart of the goddess. "What!" said she, "must I love a mortal? Alas! I feel that I adore him.—Let no more vows be paid to me at Gnidus; no deity resides there but Adonis."

It was to this place that she summoned the Loves, when, on the point of contending for the prize of beauty, she consulted them and the Graces. She was in doubt whether she should expose herself naked to the eyes of the Trojan shepherd: she hid her cestus in the tresses of her hair; her nymphs sprinkled her with perfumes; she mounted her car drawn by swans, and repaired to Phrygia. The shepherd was hesitating between Juno and Pallas when Venus appeared; he looked, his eyes wandered, they were dazzled, they became dim; the golden apple dropped from his hand, and fell at the feet of the goddess: he would have spoken; his confusion was decisive.

It was to this temple also that the young Psyche came with her mother, when Cupid, who was fluttering about

the gilded roof, found himself captivated with a look.
He felt all the pains he inflicts. "Is it thus," said he,
"that I wound? I can no longer support my bow or
my arrows." He fell on the bosom of Psyche:
"Ah!" said he, "I begin to feel that I am the god
of pleasure."

Upon entering this temple we feel a secret charm
thrilling through the heart, which it is impossible to
describe : the soul is seized with rapturous sensations,
which even the gods do not feel, except when they
approach the celestial abodes.

The gayest and most exhilarating productions of
Nature conspire with the noblest and most perfect
works of art to produce this effect.

A hand, undoubtedly immortal, has everywhere
adorned this temple with paintings that seem imbued
with life. Here is represented the birth of Venus, the
rapture of the gods when they first saw her, her confusion at finding herself naked, and that modesty which
takes precedence of all the other graces.

Here also are seen the loves of Mars and the goddess.
The painter has represented the god sitting in his
chariot, fierce and even terrible : Fame flies beside
him; Fear and Death march before his foaming
coursers. He pushes through the throng, and a cloud
of dust envelops him. On the other hand, we see him
languishingly reclining on a bed of roses : he smiles upon
Venus, and you would no longer know him but by some
features of the divinity still visible in his countenance.
The Pleasures fashion garlands, with which they bind
the two lovers; the eyes of the latter are fixed ; they

sigh ; and, entirely occupied with each other, they pay
no heed to the little Loves that flutter around them.

There is a retired apartment in which the painter has
portrayed the marriage of Venus and Vulcan.   The
whole celestial court is assembled there : the god seems
less gloomy than usual, but not less pensive.   The
goddess views the general mirth without partaking of it :
she allows her lame lover to take her hand ; he looks
as if he had stolen it ; she raises her eyes, uncertain
where to fix them ; at last she turns them towards the
Graces.

In another picture we see Juno performing the
marriage ceremony.   Venus takes the cup to swear
eternal fidelity to Vulcan, who hears her with rapture.
The gods look at one another and laugh.

In another piece we find the god who has become
impatient, seizing in his arms his divine spouse ; she
makes so much resistance that you would think she was
the daughter of Ceres, whom Pluto is about to ravish ;
—but the eye that sees Venus can never be deceived.

Farther on we view Vulcan bearing her away, to
deposit her on the nuptial couch.   The gods throng
around ; the goddess continues to resist ; she struggles,
and endeavours to escape from the arms that enfold her ;
her robe streams about her and her knees are exposed ;
but Vulcan immediately repairs this beautiful disorder,
more attentive to conceal her charms than eager to
enjoy them.

Lastly, we find the god successful ; he holds her fast
in the bed that Hymen has prepared for them : he draws
the curtains, and thinks that she is now his for ever.

The troublesome crowd at last retire ; he is delighted at their departure. The goddesses laugh, and jest, and make merry; but the gods appear thoughtful and disconsolate, and the sorrow of Mars has something dark and horrid in it, like the vengeful broodings of jealousy.

Delighted with the magnificence of the temple, the goddess has chosen it as the place where she desires to be worshipped. Here she has established rites, regulated ceremonies, and instituted festivals ; and here she is at once both deity and priestess.

The worship which is paid her, over almost the whole earth, is rather a profanation than a religion. There are temples erected to her in some cities in which all the young women prostitute themselves to her honour, and gain a dowry from the profits of their devotion. There are others, whither every married woman goes once in her life, to yield herself up to the man that chooses her, and throws into the sanctuary the money that she receives. There are others still, to which the courtesans of all countries, more honoured than the matrons, repair to offer their gifts. And, lastly, there are some where the men make themselves eunuchs, and assume the habits of women, that they may serve in the sanctuary ; dedicating to the goddess the sex they no longer possess, as well as that which they cannot acquire.

But at Gnidus she has demanded from the people a purer worship, and has instituted honours more worthy of herself. There the sacrifices are sighs and the offerings a tender heart. Each lover addresses his vows to his mistress, and Venus receives them for her.

E

Wherever beauty is found, it is adored like Venus herself; for beauty is divine like her.

Those whose hearts are full of love, come to the temple and embrace the altars of fidelity and constancy.

Those who languish under the cruelty of their mistresses come to sigh in the temple; they feel their torments alleviated, and flattering hope enters their hearts.

The goddess who has promised happiness to true lovers, always bestows it in proportion to the pangs they endure.

Jealousy is a passion which the lover may feel but which he should never show. We secretly adore the caprices of our fair tyrants, as we adore the decrees of heaven, which become just when we dare to complain of them.

The fire, the transports, and even the fury of love are reckoned among the number of the favours she bestows; for the less we are masters of our hearts, the more we are devoted to the goddess.

They who have not given away their hearts are considered as the profane, and are not permitted to enter the temple : they address their vows to the goddess from a distance, and implore her to deliver them from that liberty which is nothing but the lack of power to form desires.

The goddess inspires the young women with modesty, that charming quality which enhances the value of the treasures it conceals.

But never in these happy shades has any one blushed

for a sincere passion, for a pure sentiment, a tender confession.

The heart itself always fixes the moment for yielding; but it is profanation to yield without having loved.

Cupid is solicitous for the felicity of the Gnidians; he selects with care the arrows with which he wounds them. When he sees a forlorn fair one, sinking under the neglect of an uncomplying lover, he chooses an arrow dipped in the waters of the river of oblivion. When he finds two lovers beginning to feel the approaches of passion, he never ceases to assail them with new darts. When he meets with any whose love is beginning to decay, he either suddenly rekindles it, or allows it to expire: for he always spares the last sparks of a waning passion: and in this happy spot, love ceases without being expelled by disgust; the stronger ecstacies being past, the weaker are forgotten.

Cupid banishes from his quiver the cruel arrows with which he wounded Phedra and Ariadne; arrows which infuse hatred with love and serve to show his power as the thunder demonstrates the dominion of Jupiter.

In proportion as Cupid inspires the pleasure of loving Venus adds the delight of pleasing.

Every day the young girls enter the sanctuary to offer up their prayers to Venus. There they express sentiments as guileless as the heart that dictates them. "Queen of Amathonta!" said one of them, "the flame that once glowed in my bosom for Thirsis is extinguished: I do not ask you to rekindle it; I only implore you to grant that Ixiphilus may love me."

Another said in a low voice: "O powerful goddess!

give me resolution enough to conceal for a time my love from my shepherd, in order to enhance the value of that soft confession which I mean to make to him."

"Goddess of Cythera!" said a third, "I am pleased with solitude ; the sports of my companions no longer delight me. I am in love, perhaps. Ah! If I love, it can be none but Daphnis."

On holidays the girls and youths assemble to recite hymns in honour of Venus; they sing her praise while they relate the story of their loves.

Thus sang a young Gnidian, while he held his mistress by the hand: "O Love! when thou first beheldst Psyche, thou didst undoubtedly wound thyself with the same arrows that have now pierced my heart ; thy happiness was not different from mine, for thou didst feel the same flame that now glows in my bosom, and I rejoice in the same pleasures with which thou wast rewarded.

"I have been a witness of everything I now describe. I went to Gnidus; there I saw Themira, and I loved her : I saw her again, and I loved her still more. I will remain at Gnidus all my life with her : and I shall be the happiest of mortals.

"We will go together to the temple, and never have truer lovers crossed its threshold. We will enter the palace of Venus, and I shall believe it to be the palace of Themira ; I will hasten to the meadow, and gather flowers which I will place on her bosom ; perhaps I may persuade her to enter the grove where so many winding paths cross and intermingle ; and when I have thus led her astray—but Love, who inspires me, forbids his mysteries to be revealed."

Plate II

CANTO II.

AT Gnidus there is a sacred grotto which the nymphs inhabit, and where the goddess promulgates her oracles. There the earth does not roar under one's feet, nor does one's hair stand on end; there is no priestess as at Delphi, where Apollo agitates the Pythia: Venus herself inclines her ear to the prayers of mortals, without making a jest of their hopes or scoffing at their fears.

A coquette from the isle of Crete came once to Gnidus; whenever she appeared, the Gnidian youths flocked around her: she smiled upon one, she whispered in the ear of another, she leaned on the arm of a third, and beckoned two others to follow her. She was handsome, and dressed with taste; the sound of her voice was as delusive as her eyes. O Heavens! what cruel alarms did she not raise in the hearts of the Gnidian beauties. She presented herself to the oracle with as much confidence as if she had been a goddess;

when suddenly we heard a voice issue from the sanctuary:
" Perfidious woman, how darest thou bring thy artifices
to a place where I reign over candid hearts? I will
punish thee in an exemplary manner; I will deprive
thee of thy charms, but leave thy heart as it is;
thou shalt invite all the men as they pass, but they will
fly thee as a complaining phantom, and thou shalt
die loaded with refusals and contempt."

A courtesan of Nocretis came next, sparkling in the
spoils of her lovers. "Away!" said the goddess, "thou
art deceived if thou thinkest to increase the glory of my
empire; thy beauty shows that there are pleasures, but
it does not bestow them; thy heart is like iron; and
though thou shouldst behold my son himself, thou
couldst not feel the passion of love. Go, lavish thy
favours on the worthless who seek them, but are
soon disgusted with them; go and display those charms
that inflame but for a moment, then perish for ever!
Thou art good for nothing, but to bring my power into
contempt."

Some time after there appeared a rich man, who
levied the tribute of the King of Lydia. "You ask of
me," said the goddess, "what I cannot grant, although I
am the goddess of love. You buy mistresses that you
may love them, and you do not love them because you
buy them. Your treasures will not be altogether
useless, since they will serve to make you loathe
whatever is most enchanting and most lovely in nature."

Aristæus, a young man of Doris, next presented
himself. He had seen the charming Camilla at Gnidus,
and had conceived the most violent passion for her;

he felt the whole excess of his love, and he came to entreat Venus that she would render him still more enamoured.

"I know thy heart," said the goddess to him; "thou canst love, and I have found Camilla worthy of thee; I might have given her to the greatest king upon earth; but kings do not deserve her so well as a faithful shepherd."

It was then that I appeared with Themira. The goddess addressed me thus: "There is not in all my empire one of mortal birth so much devoted to me as thou art; but what wouldst thou have me do? I cannot make thy love more ardent, nor Themira more charming."

"Ah! great goddess," I replied, "I have a thousand favours to demand; grant that Themira may think only of me; that she may see only me; that I may be the subject of her dreams; that she may dread to lose me when I am present; that she may sigh for my return when I am absent; and that, ever happy whilst beside me, she may regret every moment that she spends without me."

CANTO III.

HERE are certain sacred games which are celebrated every year at Gnidus. Thither the women of all the neighbouring countries repair to dispute the prize of beauty. There shepherdesses are mingled with the daughters of kings, for beauty alone confers royalty. Venus presides in person; she decides without hesitation; she well knows who is the happy mortal whom she has most highly favoured.

Helen, the famous Helen, several times gained this prize. She triumphed when Theseus carried her off; she triumphed when stolen away by the son of Priam; and, lastly, she triumphed when the gods restored her to Menelaus after ten years' expectation: thus, in the judgment of Venus, this prince became as happy a husband as Theseus and Paris had been happy lovers.

Thirty of the daughters of Corinth came to Gnidus, their hair flowing in large ringlets on their shoulders.

Ten others came from Salamis, who had seen but
thirteen summers. From the Isle of Lesbos came
fifteen virgins : they said to one another, " I am all
admiration; nothing can be more charming than you
are ; if Venus saw you with my eyes, she would
crown you in the midst of all the beauties of the
universe."

There came fifty women from Miletus: nothing
could equal the fairness of their complexion, or the
regularity of their features; all presented to the eye or
to the imagination a lovely form ; and the gods who
fashioned them would never have made anything more
worthy of their art had they not sought to endow them
with perfections rather than graces.

A hundred women came from the Island of Cyprus.
" We have passed our youth," said they, " in the
temple of Venus; we have consecrated our virginity,
and even our modesty to her : we do not blush for our
charms; our manners, sometimes forward and always
free, should give us the advantage over a modesty that
is subject to continual alarms."

I saw the daughters of the proud Lacedæmon : their
robes were open at the side from the girdle downwards,
in a manner that seemed exceedingly immodest ; yet
they were prudish, and pretended that they never
violated modesty but out of love for their country.

O sea, famous for so many shipwrecks, thou art
careful to preserve the precious burdens that are sometimes entrusted to thee. Thou didst calm thy troubled
billows when the ship Argo transported the Golden
Fleece over thy watery plain: and when fifty beauties

departed from Colchis and confided themselves to thy waves, thou didst waft them safely to their destined shore.

I likewise saw Oriana, lovely as a goddess: all the beauties of Lydia surrounded their queen. She had sent before her a hundred virgins, who had presented to Venus an offering of two hundred talents. Candaules, too, was there, more distinguished by his love than by the purple of royalty. He spent day and night in devouring the charms of Oriana with his eyes which wandered over her lovely person, and never wearied of contemplating her. "Alas!" said he, "I am happy, but my happiness is known only to Venus and myself; it would be increased if it created envy. Fair queen, quit those vain ornaments, throw aside that envious veil and show yourself to the universe; leave the contest for the prize of beauty, and claim what is thy due, altars and adoration."

At a little distance were assembled twenty Babylonian women arrayed in robes of purple embroidered with gold. They supposed that the magnificence of their apparel would enhance their own value. Some of them indeed bore, as a proof of their beauty, the riches it had enabled them to acquire.

At a greater distance I beheld a hundred women from the plains of Egypt. They had black eyes and jet black hair; their husbands attended them, and said: "The laws have made us subject to you in honour of Isis; but your beauty has acquired a dominion over us, much stronger than that of the laws: we yield obedience to you with as much pleasure as we pay it to the gods: we are the happiest slaves in the universe ; our duty assures you of our fidelity ; but to Love alone are we indebted for yours.

" Be less sensible to the glory which you acquire at Gnidus, than to the homage which is paid you at home by a submissive husband ; who, whilst you are occupied abroad, waits with patience, in the bosom of your family, for the heart you vouchsafe to give him."

There came women from that powerful city which sends its ships from one end of the earth to the other. Their heads were scarcely able to support the variety of ornaments with which they were loaded ; and every quarter of the world seemed to have contributed to adorn them.

Ten beauties came from the regions which the sun first irradiates with his early beams : they were daughters of Aurora ; and in order to behold her, they arose every day before her. They complained of the sun, who made their mother disappear ; they complained of their mother, who never showed herself to them otherwise than she appears to the rest of the world.

Under a tent I saw the queen of a nation of the Indies ; she was surrounded by her daughters, who already promised to equal their mother in beauty. She was served by eunuchs whose eyes were cast sorrowfully on the ground : for, ever since they had breathed the air of Gnidus, they had felt the whole misery of their condition, and their fearful melancholy had redoubled.

The women of Cadiz, who live at the extremity of the earth, likewise contended for the prize. There is

no country in the world in which a beautiful woman
does not meet with admiration : but nothing short of
the greatest homage can content the ambition of a
beauty.

At last appeared the daughters of Gnidus, beautiful
in simplicity, exhibiting their graces instead of pearls and
rubies. The presents of Flora were the only ornaments
upon their heads; but they were thereby rendered the
more worthy of the embraces of Zephyrus. Their robes
had no other merit than that of displaying an elegant
shape, and of being wrought by their own hands.

Amongst all these beauties Camilla was not to be
seen. She had said : " I will not contend for the prize
of beauty; it is enough for me that I should appear lovely
in the eyes of my dear Aristæus."

Diana added fame to these games by her presence.
She did not come to dispute the prize ; for the goddesses
do not contend with mortals. I saw her alone : she
seemed as beautiful as Venus; I saw her afterwards by
the side of Venus, and I acknowledged that she was
only Diana.

Never was there so magnificent a spectacle. The
people of every different nation were assembled ; the eye
wandered from country to country, from the eastern
mountains to the western sea; it appeared as if
Gnidus were the universe.

The gods have distributed beauty among the nations,
as nature has divided it among the goddesses. Here
you might see the noble beauty of Pallas, there the
grandeur and majesty of Juno, at a little distance
the simplicity of Diana, the delicacy of Thetis, the

attractions of the Graces, and sometimes the smile of Venus.

The women of each different nation seemed to entertain different notions of modesty, but they were all inclined to sport with the eyes of beholders. Some of them displayed the neck and concealed the shoulders, while others exhibited the shoulders and hid the neck. Those who covered the foot repaid you with the sight of other charms; and there one blushed at what another considered to be authorised by decency itself.

The gods are so charmed with Themira, that they never behold her without a smile of complacency and congratulation on their own work. But of the goddesses Venus is the only one who views her with pleasure, and whom the gods do not rally for an inclination to jealousy.

As a rose is remarked among the flowers of the field, so was Themira distinguished among the beauties assembled at Gnidus. They had not time to become her rivals; they were conquered before they began to dread her. No sooner did she appear than Venus looked at none but her. She summoned the Graces: "Go and crown her," said the goddess; "of all the beauties before me she alone resembles you."

CANTO IV.

DURING the time that Themira was employed with her companions in the worship of the goddess, I entered a solitary wood, where I found the tender Aristæus. We had seen each other for the first time on the day when we went to consult the oracle: it was enough to engage us in conversation; for Venus inspires the heart, in the presence of an inhabitant of Gnidus, with that secret charm which is felt by two friends, when, after a tedious absence, they receive into their arms the dear object of their solicitude.

Delighted with each other, we felt that our hearts were akin; the genius of friendship seemed to have descended from heaven, to have taken a place between us. We related, by turns, a thousand incidents of our lives, and this is what I said to him :—

" I was born at Sybaris, where my father Antilochus was the priest of Venus. In that city no difference is

made between voluptuous pleasures and necessities ; all the arts are banished that might disturb gentle sleep ; a reward is given at the expense of the state to those who can invent a new pleasure. The citizens retain only the memory of the buffoons who have amused them, and quickly lose all remembrance of the magistrates who have governed them.

" The soil produces an eternal abundance, but its fertility is abused ; the favours of the gods bestowed on Sybaris serve only to encourage luxury and foster sloth.

" The men are so effeminate ; their apparel is so like that of the women ; they take so much care of their complexion ; they dress their hair with so much art ; they waste so much time at their toilet, that you would think there was only one sex in the city.

" The women cannot be said to yield, for they make no resistance whatever ; each day sees the hopes and the desires of each day conceived and accomplished : the pleasure of loving and of being loved is unknown ; and what is so falsely called enjoyment is the only occupation.

" Favours there have nothing but their own intrinsic value ; all those circumstances that so naturally accompany them, all those nothings that are valued so highly, those engagements that always appear of such consequence, those little things that seem so great, everything which paves the way for the happy moment, so many conquests preparatory to the great one, so many enjoyments previous to the last, all are unknown at Sybaris.

" Still, if they were possessed of the smallest portion of modesty, that feeble image of virtue might please ;

but, alas! the eyes are accustomed to see everything without a veil, and the ears to hear everything without concealment.

" This multiplicity of pleasures, far from inspiring the Sybarites with greater delicacy, renders them incapable of distinguishing one sentiment from another.

" They pass their lives in purely sensual enjoyments; they quit one pleasure of which they are tired for another pleasure which will also soon disappoint them. Whatever wish their imagination forms is but a new subject of disgust.

" Their souls, incapable of the sentiment of pleasure, seem only alive to the impression of pain: a citizen was unable to rest the whole night long from a rose having been folded under him in his bed.

" Effeminacy has so debilitated their frames that they are unable to move the smallest weight; they can hardly support themselves on their limbs; the motion of the easiest carriage makes them swoon; and, at feasts, their appetites fail them, and their stomachs reject the most delicate food.

" They pass their lives on the softest couches, upon which they are obliged to repose the whole day long, without the excuse of fatigue; they are bruised and hurt when they recline on anything harder.

" They are incapable of bearing the weight of arms; they are timid before their fellow citizens, cowardly before strangers, and accordingly they are destined to be the slaves of the first master who may come to conquer them.

" No sooner was I able to exercise the faculty of

reason than I became disgusted with this miserable
Sybaris. I love virtue, and have always feared the
immortal gods. 'No,' said I, 'I will no longer breathe
this tainted air; these slaves of effeminacy are made
for living in their native country, I for quitting it.'

"I repaired for the last time to the temple; and
approaching the altar where my father had so often
sacrificed: 'Great goddess!' cried I in a loud voice, 'I
abandon thy temple, but not thy worship : in whatever
place of the world I may be, I will never fail to burn
incense at thy shrine; but it shall be purer than that
which is offered to thee at Sybaris!'

"I departed, and arrived in Crete. That island is
filled with monuments of the madness of love. There is
preserved the brazen bull, the workmanship of Dædalus,
invented to deceive or to satisfy the corrupt desires of
Pasiphæ; the labyrinth of which Cupid alone could
elude the artifices still exists there; there is the tomb
of a Phedra, who made the sun start back as her mother
had done; and there too is the temple of Ariadne, who,
though left alone in a desert, and abandoned by a false
and ungrateful lover, did not repent of having followed
him.

"There is seen the palace of Idomeneus, whose return
was happier than that of the other Grecian leaders : for
those who escaped the dangers of an outrageous element,
found their own homes still more fatal. Venus, enraged,
led them to embrace perfidious wives, and they perished
by the hands they most tenderly loved.

"I quitted that island, so odious to a goddess, who
was soon to bring about the felicity of my life.

"I embarked, and a tempest threw me on Lesbos. That also is an island but little favoured by Venus: she has banished modesty from the faces of the women, delicacy from their frames, and timidity from their souls. O powerful Venus! let the women of Lesbos burn with a legitimate flame; and preserve human nature from a sight of so much horror!

"Mitylene is the capital of Lesbos; it is the native city of the tender Sappho. Immortal as the Muses, this ill-fated maiden burns with a fire she is unable to extinguish. Odious to herself, and finding subject of chagrin in her own charms, she hates her sex, though for ever in pursuit of it. 'Alas!' said she, 'can so vain a passion be so cruel? O love! thou art a thousand times more terrible in thy sports than in thy rage.'

"At last I quitted Lesbos, and chance led me to an island yet more profane, that of Lemnos. Venus has here no temple: the Lemnians never address a single vow to her. 'We reject,' say they, 'a worship which enervates the heart.' The goddess has often punished them for this impiety, and they suffer the punishment without expiating their crime; growing always more impious as they are more afflicted.

"I again committed myself to the sea, ever seeking some country favoured by the gods: the winds carried me to Delos. I remained for some months in that sacred island: but whether the gods inspire us sometimes with a foresight of what is to happen to us, or whether our souls retain a portion of the divinity from which they emanate, some slight knowledge of futurity, I

found that my destiny, that my happiness itself, called
me to another climate.

"One night, when I was in that state of tranquillity
in which the soul, more master of itself, seems detached
from the chain which holds it captive, there appeared
to me a female form, I knew not at first whether of
mortal or of celestial origin. A secret charm was
diffused over this being's person; she was not so beautiful
as Venus, but like her she was alluring : all her features
were not regular, but combined they were enchanting;
you did not find in her so much of that which is admired
as of that which stirs the senses : her hair fell negli-
gently over her shoulders, but that negligence was felicitous : her shape was elegant, she possessed that air
which nature alone can give, and the secret of which she
conceals even from the most masterly painters. The
apparition saw my astonishment, and smiled at it.
Ye gods, what a smile !

"'I am,' she said to me, in a voice that thrilled my
heart; 'the second of the Graces : Venus, by whose
orders I appear, means to render you happy, but you
must go to worship her in her temple at Gnidus.' She
disappeared ; my arms were stretched out to detain her ;
but my dream vanished, and nothing remained save a
soft regret at seeing her no more, mingled with the
pleasure of having seen her.

"I accordingly left the island of Delos, and I arrived
at Gnidus. I can affirm, that the moment I landed I
drew in at every breath the sweet passion of love : I
felt—but I cannot express what I felt : I was not as yet
in love, but I wished to be so ; my heart warmed as in

the presence of some divine beauty. I advanced, and
saw at a little distance some young girls who were
sporting in a meadow; I was at once irresistibly
drawn towards them. 'Madman that thou art!' said I
to myself; 'without being in love, thy soul is agitated
with all the transports which attend that passion : thy
heart already flies to unknown objects, and those objects
already give it inquietude. I approached; I beheld the
charming Themira ; no doubt we must have been made
for each other ; my eyes constantly dwelt upon her, and
I think I should have died had she not now and then
turned hers also upon me. 'Great Venus!' cried I,
'since thou hast promised to make me happy, grant
that it may be with this shepherdess : I renounce every
other beauty ; she alone will I accept as the accomplish-
ment of your promise, and of all the wishes I shall ever
form.'"

CANTO V.

thus told the young Aristæus the story of my love; it made him sigh for his own; I wished to pour consolation into his heart, by begging him to relate to me in his turn the story of his passion. The following is what he told me: I have not forgotten a word of it, for I am inspired by the same god that made him speak.

"Throughout my recital," said he, "you will find nothing but simple occurrences; my adventures are only the sentiments of a tender heart: nothing but my pleasures and my pains; and as my love for Camilla forms all the happiness, so does it form all the history of my life.

"Camilla is the daughter of one of the principal inhabitants of Gnidus: she is beautiful, but she is endowed with graces more captivating than beauty itself: she has a look which instantly penetrates the heart of every beholder: women, when they wish for beauty, demand from the gods the graces of Camilla; the men who see her long to gaze upon her for ever, or dread to see her again.

" She has a charming figure, a noble, but modest air, lively eyes, that seem formed for the expression of tenderness and sensibility; the most regular features; and, in a word, an assemblage of charms inexpressibly fitted to hold every heart in subjection.

" Camilla is not solicitous about her dress; but she is always better dressed than other women.

" She has a mind such as nature nearly always denies to women whose persons have been formed to please. She is equally disposed to thoughtfulness and gaiety: if you are serious, she will discourse to you like Pallas; if merry, she becomes as sprightly as the Graces.

" The more wit one has, the more one finds in Camilla. There is so much native simplicity in her thoughts, that her words are always the language of her heart: whatever she says, whatever she does, has this charm: you will always find her the simple shepherdess; but one whose gentle, refined, and delicate graces never fail to be observed, never fail to be felt.

" With all this, Camilla loves me: she is happy when she sees me; she becomes sorrowful when I leave her: and, as if I could exist without her, she makes me promise to return. I am ever telling her how much I love her, and she believes me; I say that I adore her, and she knows it; but she is as delighted with my assurances as if she heard them for the first time. I tell her that she constitutes the happiness of my life;

she replies, that I am all her felicity: in a word, she loves me so much, that she makes me almost believe myself worthy of her love.

" I had opportunities of seeing Camilla during a whole month before I dared to tell her that I loved her, and even scarcely dared to tell it to myself: the more amiable I found her, the less did I hope to be the happy man who would make an impression on her heart. Camilla! I was sensible to thy charms, but they proclaimed that I was not worthy of thee!

" I sought by every means to forget thee; I wanted to efface thy adorable image from my heart: how happy I am that my efforts were ineffectual; there that image still remains, and it shall never be erased.

" I said to Camilla, 'I once was fond of the bustle of the world, but now I court solitude: my soul glowed with ambition, and now my only wish is thy presence: I longed to range through foreign countries, but now my heart abides solely in the place which you inhabit: you are the only object that my eyes desire, or that my heart covets.'

" When Camilla talks to me of her love, she even has something more to say: she thinks she has forgotten to tell me what she has sworn to me a thousand times. I am so charmed with listening to her, that I sometimes feign not to believe her, that she may still continue to touch my heart: and soon our discourse gives place to that sweet silence which is the tenderest eloquence of lovers.

" When I have been absent from Camilla, I begin to give her an account of the things I may have seen or

heard. ' What are these things to me ? ' she will say :
' if you would entertain me, talk to me only of our love ;
but if your imagination suggest nothing to you, if you
have nothing to say on the subject, cruel man ! then
let me speak.'

"Sometimes, throwing her arms around me, 'You
are melancholy,' she will say. ' It is true,' I reply ;
' but the melancholy of lovers is luxurious ; I feel my
tears flow, and I know not why, for thou lovest me :
I have no cause of complaint, and yet I complain.
Ah ! do not seek to disturb this soft languor ; allow
me to sigh at both my pleasures and my pains.

"' In the transports of love my soul is too greatly
agitated : it is hurried towards its happiness, without
enjoying it ; but at present my very sorrow is voluptuous ; do not wipe away my tears ; what matters it
though I weep, provided I am happy.'

"Sometimes Camilla says to me, 'Dost thou love
me ?' 'Yes, I love thee.' 'But how dost thou love
me ?' 'Alas !' I say, 'I love thee now as I loved
thee before ; for I can only compare the love I now
feel to that I have formerly felt.'

"I hear the praises of Camilla resound from the lips
of all who know her. I am flattered with these praises
as if they were my own, and I feel at that moment how
selfish I am.

"When there is any one beside us, she speaks with
so much wit that I am enchanted with her most
ordinary expressions ; but I rather wish she were
silent.

"When she does a favour to any one, I wish I were

the person on whom she confers that favour, when suddenly I reflect that then I should not be the person she loves.

" 'Beware, O Camilla! of the deceitfulness of lovers ; they will tell you that they love, and they will tell you the truth ; they will say that they love you as much as I do; but I swear to you, by the gods, that I love you most.'

" When I behold her at a distance, my spirits are inflamed ; when she draws near, my heart is agitated : I approach her, and my soul seems ready to quit me ; seems to belong only to Camilla, and she appears ready to animate it.

"Sometimes, when I want to snatch a favour from her, she refuses it, but an instant later grants me another : this is not the effect of artifice—struggling at once with her modesty and her love, she wishes to refuse me everything, and yet she wishes she could grant me all.

" She says to me, ' Is it not enough that I love you ? What can you desire when you possess my heart ? '— ' I desire,' I reply, ' that, for my sake, you will consent to commit a fault which love always prompts to, and which powerful love always justifies.'

" 'Camilla! if ever I cease to love you, may the Fates make a mistake, and, thinking that moment the last of my existence, cut the fatal thread! may they efface the remainder of a life which I should find insupportable when I reflected on the pleasures I enjoyed in loving you.' "

Aristæus sighed and was silent ; and I plainly saw that he only ceased to speak of Camilla in order that he might occupy his mind in thinking of her.

H

CANTO VI.

HILE we were thus talking of our loves, we had strayed from the road, and after we had wandered about for some time, we entered a spacious meadow. We were conducted by a path strewed with flowers to the foot of a fearful rock : we saw a dark cavern; we entered it, thinking it the habitation of some mortal. O gods! who would have thought that such a place had been so fatal! Scarcely had I set my foot within the entrance, than I felt my whole frame tremble; my hair stood on end; an invisible hand dragged me into the dread abode; and in proportion as my heart was agitated, it grew desirous of further agitation. " Friend," cried I, " let us proceed, though every step should augment our uneasiness." I accordingly advanced into this place, where the sun had never entered, and which the winds never refresh. I there saw Jealousy; her aspect was more sullen than

Tab. 11

Car. Visan del N. le Mire Sculp

terrrible; paleness, and sorrow, and silence surrounded her; and languor and lethargy hovered about. She breathed upon us, she placed her hand upon our hearts, she struck us on the head, and we saw nothing, our imaginations presented nothing to us but monsters. "Enter farther," said she, "unhappy mortals! proceed farther, and you will find a goddess more powerful than I." We saw a frightful deity by the light of the flames that issued from the mouths of a hundred serpents which hissed upon her head. This was Frenzy. She unloosed one of the serpents, and threw him on to me: I would have caught him; but, before I perceived it, he had slid into my heart. I remained for a moment confounded; but, as soon as the poison entered into my veins, I thought myself engulphed in the horrors of hell: my soul was on fire, and moved to such violence that my body could scarcely restrain it. I thought myself abandoned to the scourge of the Furies. At last I gave myself up to despair: we went round and round this horrible cavern a hundred times: we passed from Jealousy to Frenzy, and from Frenzy to Jealousy: we cried "Themira!" we cried "Camilla!" If Themira or Camilla had come to our call, we should have torn them to pieces with our own hands.

At last we escaped, and beheld the light of day; it appeared offensive to our eyes, and we almost regretted the frightful cave we had just quitted. We fell down from sheer fatigue, but repose itself seemed insupportable to us: our eyes refused us the consolation of tears, and our hearts were incapable of heaving a single sigh.

I was however for a moment calm : Sleep began to
shed his sweet poppies over my eyes. O ye gods!
how cruel even this sleep became! Images presented
themselves to my imagination more terrible to me than
the ghosts of the dead : I awoke every instant with the
idea of Themira's infidelity: I saw her—no, I dare not
even reflect on it; and what I had only imagined
before, I now found realised in the horrors of that sleep.

" Must I then," said I as I awoke, " fly the darkness
as well as the light ? Themira, cruel Themira agitates
me like the Furies. Who could have imagined that my
happiness would consist in forgetting her for ever."

Another fit of frenzy assailed me. " Friend," said I,
" arise ; let us go and exterminate the flocks which feed
in this meadow ; let us pursue those shepherds whose
lives are so peaceful. But no ; I see a temple at a
distance ; it is perhaps the temple of Love; let us go
and raze it to the foundations; let us break Love's
statue, and make our fury dreadful to him." We ran,
and you would have thought that our eagerness to
commit a crime had given us fresh strength. We
traversed the woods, the meads, and the fields ; we
stopped not an instant ; a hill vainly rose before us ; we
at once ascended it, and entered the temple. It was
consecrated to Bacchus. How great is the power of
the gods ! our frenzy was instantly calmed. We looked
at each other, and with astonishment beheld the disorder
in which we were involved.

" Great god ! " cried I, " I give thee thanks, not so
much that thou hast appeased my fury, as that thou
hast withheld me from committing a great crime."

And approaching the priestess, " We are favoured by the god whom you serve; he has calmed the dreadful transports with which we were agitated; scarcely had we entered this sacred place, than we experienced his instant favour; we wish to offer him a sacrifice; deign to present it for us, divine priestess ! " Then I went and sought for a victim, and laid it at her feet.

While the priestess was preparing to deal the fatal stroke, Aristæus pronounced these words : " Divine Bacchus! thou dost delight to see joy upon the human countenance; our pleasures are the worship thou requirest; and thou dost only desire the adoration of the happiest mortals.

" Sometimes thou dost gently lead our reason astray; but when some cruel divinity has bereft us of it entirely, it is thou alone that canst restore it.

" Black jealousy, that horrid fiend, holds Love in bondage; but thou rescuest our hearts from the empire she exercises over them, and compellest her to retreat within her fearful abode."

After the sacrifice had been performed, all the people flocked around us; and I was relating to the priestess how we had been tortured in the habitation of Jealousy, when all at once we heard a great noise, and a confused mingling of voices and instruments of music. We issued from the temple, and saw approaching a troop of Bacchantes who struck the ground with their thirsi, crying with a loud voice, "Evohe, evohe!" Old Silenus was in the rear, mounted on his ass; his head seemed to seek the ground; and whenever his escort ceased to support his body, it rocked from side to side

as if it beat time to music. The whole troop had their
faces besmeared with wine lees. Pan next appeared
with his flute, and the satyrs surrounded their king.
Joy reigned in the midst of confusion ; and sport and
raillery, the dance and the song, were mingled together
in happy delirium ; the wine disposed the satyrs to
mirth, and mirth again enticed them to wine. At length
I saw Bacchus : he was seated in his car drawn by
tigers, even as the Ganges, at the extremity of the
universe, beheld him, when he appeared in his glory,
spreading joy and victory on every hand.

At his side was the beautiful Ariadne.   Fair princess !
you were still lamenting the infidelity of the cruel
Theseus, when the god took your crown and placed it
in heaven.   He wiped the tears from your eyes : ah !
if you had not ceased to weep, you would have rendered
a god still more unhappy than yourself, who were but a
mortal.   " Love me," he said ; " Theseus has fled from
you ; think of his love no more ; forget even his perfidy.
I make you immortal, that I may love you for ever."

I saw Bacchus descend from his car ; I saw Ariadne
descend, and enter into the temple.   "Amiable god ! "
cried she, " let us remain in this charming place, and
here let us sigh out our loves ; let us command that
eternal joy shall abide in this happy climate.   It is near
this place that the queen of hearts has established her
dominion ; let the god of joy reign beside her, and
augment the felicity of a people already so highly
favoured.

" For myself, divine Bacchus, I already feel my love
increased : who would have thought that you could one

day appear still more amiable in my eyes? The immortals alone are capable of loving to excess, of loving still more and more: they alone obtain pleasures that exceed their hopes, and are more moderate in their desires than in their enjoyments.

" You shall here be the object of my eternal passion. In heaven we are occupied with nothing but our glory, it is only upon earth and in these rural solitudes that true love is to be found : and whilst this troop gives way to its intemperate delight, my joy, my sighs, nay, my very tears shall incessantly tell you of my love."

The god smiled on Ariadne, and led her to the sanctuary. Joy took possession of our hearts; we felt a divine emotion : infected by the transports of Silenus and the Bacchantes, we each seized a thyrsus, and mingled in the dances and the concert.

CANTO VII.

VENTUALLY we quitted the place consecrated to Bacchus; but we soon began to imagine that our miseries had only been suspended. It is true that we no longer felt the frenzy with which we had been agitated; but sadness and melancholy had taken possession of our souls, and we were tortured with suspicions and inquietude.

We imagined that the cruel goddesses in the gloomy cavern had inflicted this suffering upon us to give us a foretaste of the miseries to which we were destined.

Sometimes we regretted the temple of Bacchus; but soon we were attracted towards that of Gnidus : we wished to see Themira and Camilla, those powerful objects of our love and our jealousy.

But we felt none of those sweet sensations which it is usual to feel when, after a long absence, and on the point of again seeing the beloved object, the soul

already experiences delight and enjoys a foretaste of all the happiness it has promised itself.

" Perhaps," said Aristæus, " I shall find the shepherd Lycas with Camilla; how do I know but that he is speaking to her at this moment? O ye gods ! the false one listens to him with pleasure ! "

" It was said the other day," replied I, " that Thirsis, who was once so enamoured of Themira, was about to return to Gnidus.   He loved her once ! undoubtedly he must love her still ; and I shall be forced to dispute a heart that I had fondly believed was wholly mine."

" The other day Lycas sang in praise of my Camilla : O fool that I was ! I was charmed at hearing him praise her."

" I remember that Thirsis brought some new-blown flowers to my Themira : unhappy mortal that I am ! she put them in her bosom ! ' They are a present from Thirsis,' said she.   Ah ! I ought to have torn them away, and trampled them under my feet."

" Not long ago, I went with Camilla to sacrifice two turtle doves to Venus, when suddenly they escaped from me, and flew away."

" I had written my name and that of Themira on a tree ; I had carved on it the story of our loves ; I read that story again and again, and was never tired of reading it ; but one morning I found it all effaced."

" Do not, Camilla, do not drive to despair an un-happy man who loves you ; love when it is outraged may produce all the effects of hatred."

" The first Gnidian youth that dares to look at my Themira I will pursue even into the temple ; and I will

I

punish him though he take refuge at the feet of Venus
herself."

Whilst we were thus venting our jealousy we arrived
at the sacred grotto where the goddess pronounces her
oracles.   The people appeared like the waves of the
agitated ocean.   Some had just received, and others
were   hastening   to   receive   an   answer   to   their
petitions.

We entered with the crowd.   I lost the happy
Aristæus ; he had already embraced his Camilla, whilst
I was still in search of my Themira.

At last I found her : I felt my jealousy redouble when
I beheld her ; I felt my former frenzy rekindle ; but she
looked at me, and I became calm : thus the Furies,
when they have issued from hell, instantly fly back at
the sight of a god.

" O heaven," cried she, " how many tears have you
cost me ! three times has the sun performed his course ;
I thought I had lost you for ever."   These words made
me tremble.   " I came to consult the oracle ; I did not
ask if you loved me, I only wished to know if you were
alive : Venus has just given me an answer ; she has
declared that your love is undiminished."

" Excuse," said I, " an unfortunate man who might
have hated you, had his soul been capable of it.   The
gods, in whose hands I am, may take from me the
faculty of reason ; but no god can prevent me from
loving you.

" I have been agitated by cruel jealousy as the guilty
shades are tormented in Tartarus : but I derive this
advantage from it, that I am more sensible of the

happiness of being loved by you, since the frightful situation in which I found myself from the fear of losing you.

" Come, then, Themira, come with me into the
solitary woods, and let me expiate my crime by showing
the ardour of my love ; for it was a great crime, Themira,
to believe you false."

Never were the woods of Elysium which the gods have
planted for the tranquillity of the shades they love ;
never were the forests of Dodona that discourse to
mortals of their future felicity ; never were the gardens
of the Hesperides where the trees bend to the earth
under the weight of golden fruit ; never were any of
these so delightful as that hallowed grove, made
voluptuous by the presence of Themira !

I remember that a satyr who was pursuing a nymph,
who fled from him all in tears, saw us and stopped.
" Happy lovers ! " cried he, "your eyes understand and
reply to each other ; your sighs are repaid with sighs !
whilst I waste my days in pursuing a coy nymph,
unhappy whilst I pursue, and still more unhappy when
I have overtaken her."

A young nymph, wandering alone in the wood, also
perceived us and sighed. " No," said she, " it is only
to augment my distress that cruel Cupid has shown me
so tender a lover."

We found Apollo seated on the brink of a fountain.
He was following Diana, whom a timid doe had
seduced into the wood. I knew him by his golden
hair and by the retinue of immortals that surrounded
him. He tuned his lyre ; it attracted the rocks ; the
trees ranged themselves around it, and the lions became

motionless; but we penetrated still farther into the forest, solicited in vain by this heavenly harmony.

Where do you think I found the little god of love? I found him on the lips of Themira; I found him afterwards in her bosom: he took refuge at her feet, and I pursued him thither; he hid himself amid the folds of her garments and I followed him; and I would have followed him still, had not Themira all in tears, Themira angry and alarmed, withheld me: the god had found a secure retreat, which proved so charming that he could not quit it. Thus the tender redbreast, whom fear and love retain upon her young, remains motionless under the eager hand that approaches, and cannot resolve to abandon them.

Unhappy being that I am! Themira heard my complaints, and was not touched with them. She heard my prayers, but continued inexorable; at last I became rash, she grew angry; I trembled, and she seemed vexed; she thrust me away, I fell to the ground; and I became sensible that my sighs would have been the last of my life had not Themira laid her hand upon my heart, and revived me.

"No," said she, "I am not so cruel as you are; for I never desired to make you die, whereas you wish to drag me to the night of the grave.

"Open those dying eyes, if you do not wish that mine should close for ever."

She embraced me, and I received my pardon, but, alas, without the hope of becoming guilty!

Car. Vanon del.

S. le More Sculp.

CEPHISA
AND CUPID.

NE day as I was straying in the woods of Idalia with the young Cephisa, I stumbled upon Cupid, who lay sleeping on the flowers beneath a few branches of myrtle that gently yielded to the breath of the zephyrs. The little Smiles and Sports, that are ever in his train, had gone to frolic at a distance, and he was alone. I had him in my power; his bow and his quiver were at his side; and if I had chosen I might have stolen the arms of Cupid. Cephisa seized the bow of the greatest of the gods: she fixed in it an arrow, without my perceiving her, and shot it at me. I smiled, and said to her.

" Take another, Cephisa, and give me another wound; that is too gentle."

She was preparing another arrow when it fell upon her foot, and she gave a slight cry; it was the heaviest arrow in the quiver of love. She took it up, and let it fly at me: it struck me and I was conquered.

" Ah ! Cephisa ! are you resolved then on my death ! "

She drew near to Cupid. " He sleeps soundly," said she; " he is fatigued with shooting his arrows; we must gather flowers and tie his hands and feet—"

"Ah! I can never consent to that," said I, " for he has always favoured us."

" I will take his weapons then," said she, " and shoot at him with all my strength.—"

" But he will awake," said I.

" Let him," she replied; " what can he do but wound us still more ? "

" No, no, let him lie there ; we will remain near him, and we shall feel our flame increase."

Cephisa then took some roses and myrtle leaves : " I will cover him with these," said she ; " and the Smiles and the Sports will seek for him but will not find him."

She strewed them over him, and she laughed to see the little god almost buried. " But why am I trifling ? " said she. " I must cut his wings, that there may no longer be any false and fickle men in the world; for the little god flies from heart to heart, and plants levity and inconstancy everywhere."

She sat down, she took out her scissors, and held with one hand the tips of Love's gilded pinions. I felt my heart shrink for fear.

" Stop, Cephisa."

She heard me not; she cut off the tips of Cupid's wings, let fall her scissors, and ran away.

When Cupid awoke he wished to fly, but felt a weight which was new to him : he saw the tips of his wings lying upon the flowers and began to weep.

Jupiter, observing him from the summit of Olympus, sent a cloud which carried him to the palace of Gnidus, and laid him in the lap of Venus.

"Mother," said he, "I used to flutter with my wings on your bosom; but they have been cut, alas, and what will become of me!"

"My son," said the fair Cypris, "do not weep; stay where you are, do not move from my bosom, its heat will make your pinions grow again; do you not already see that they are longer?—Kiss me;—they grow; you will soon have them as they were before;—now I see the tips acquiring their golden colour again—in another instant—enough, fly, fly, my child."

"Yes," said he, "I will venture."

He flew; he lighted at her side; but instantly returned to her bosom. He resumed his flight, he settled at a greater distance, and again returned to the bosom of Venus. He embraced her, she smiled upon him: he embraced her again and toyed with her: at last he rose into the air, whence he now reigns over all nature.

Cupid, to be revenged of Cephisa, has made her the most fickle of the fair. He makes her burn every day with a new flame. She loved me; she loved Daphnis, and now she loves Cleon. Cruel Cupid! it is I you punish. I am willing to suffer for her crime, but may you not have other torments to afflict me with?

ARSACES
AND
ISMENIA.
AN EASTERN STORY

"Arsaces go & tell your new spouse that
I am dead"

ARSACES AND ISMENIA.

EAR the close of the reign of Artamenes, Bactra was harassed with
civil broils. The king, overwhelmed
with care, died, and left the throne
to his daughter Ismenia. Aspar,
chief of the royal eunuchs, had the
principal management of affairs. He was anxious
for the prosperity of the kingdom, but by no means for
power. He knew mankind, and could judge with some
certainty of events. He was naturally inclined to con-
ciliatory measures ; indeed his heart seemed to cleave
to the human race. Peace at length was unexpectedly
established ; and, such was the influence of Aspar, that
everyone returned to his duty almost without knowing
that he had departed from it ; for without bustle or
ostentation the minister was able to perform great
things.

The peace was disturbed by the King of Hircania,
who sent ambassadors to demand Ismenia in marriage ;

K

and, upon being refused, marched into Bactra. His
approach was singular. Sometimes he appeared armed
at all points, and ready to encounter his enemies:
sometimes he was seen habited like a lover whom Cupid
is conducting to his mistress. He carried with him all
that was necessary for a wedding; such as dancers,
musicians, players, cooks, eunuchs, and women; and
he also brought with him a formidable army. He wrote
the most tender letters to the queen; and he ravaged
the whole country: one day was spent in feasting, the
next in military expeditions. Never had such a perfect
representation of war and peace been seen; never so
much dissipation, nor so much discipline: one village
fled from the cruelty of the conqueror; another was all
joy, merriment, and riot: for, by a strange caprice, he
strove to attain two things that are incompatible: he
wished to be feared, and at the same time loved. But
he was neither feared nor loved. An army was sent to
oppose him, and a single battle finished the war. A
soldier who had lately joined the Bactrian army
performed prodigies of valour. He penetrated to the
place where the King of Hircania was fighting bravely,
and took him prisoner. He gave this prince in
charge to an officer; and without telling his name, fell
back into the ranks, but he was followed by acclamations, and led in triumph to the general's tent. He
appeared before the general with a noble boldness; and
spoke with modesty of his exploit. The general offered
him rewards, but he appeared insensible to them;
honours would have been heaped upon him, but with
these he seemed familiar,

Aspar judged that such a man could not be of ordinary birth. He invited him to Court, and, when he saw him, he was still more confirmed in his opinion. His figure struck the eunuch with admiration; even the melancholy that appeared on his countenance inspired him with respect. Aspar praised his valour, and said the most civil things to him.

"Sir," responded the stranger, "forgive an unhappy man, if the dreadful state of his mind renders him almost incapable of feeling your kindness, or of making any return to it."

Tears then rushed into his eyes, and the eunuch was moved.

"Be my friend," said he, "if you are unfortunate. A few moments ago I admired you; but now my admiration is changed into love. I wish to console you; perhaps my counsel may not be useless to you. Accept of an apartment in my palace, its owner loves virtue, and you will not be a stranger there."

The next day was a festival over all Bactra. The queen issued from her palace, followed by the whole Court. She appeared in her chariot in the midst of an immense multitude of people. A veil covered her face, but allowed the elegance of her shape to appear; her countenance was concealed, but the affection of her people pictured it in imagination.

She descended from her chariot and entered the temple. The nobles of Bactra surrounded her. She prostrated herself, and adored the gods in silence; then raising her veil, she solemnly pronounced the following words :—

"Immortal gods! the Queen of Bactra comes to thank you for the victory with which you have crowned her arms. Fill up the measure of your bounties, by granting that she may not abuse them. May she be neither the slave of passions, nor of weakness, nor caprice; may all her fears be to commit evil, all her desires to do good : and, since she cannot be happy," continued she, in a voice interrupted by sobbing, " at least grant that her people may be so."

The priests having finished the ceremonies prescribed for the worship of the gods, the queen left the temple, mounted her chariot, and was followed by the people to the gates of the palace.

A little while after, Aspar went home, and enquiring for the stranger found him plunged in the deepest melancholy. He sat down beside him, and having ordered the attendants to withdraw, " I conjure you," said he, " to unbosom yourself to me. Do you think that a troubled heart finds no relief in imparting its sorrows to another ? We then seem to enjoy a state of more tranquillity."

" It would be necessary," said the stranger, " to relate to you all the events of my life."

" That is exactly what I wish," replied Aspar; " you will speak to a man who is not devoid of sensibility : conceal nothing from him ; everything is of importance in the eyes of friendship."

It was not merely sympathy and a sentiment of pity that excited the curiosity of Aspar; he wished to attach this extraordinary man to the Court of Bactra and was eager to become thoroughly acquainted with a person whom in his thoughts he already associated in his schemes and destined to great affairs.

The stranger meditated for a moment, and then began :—

" Love brought about all the happiness and all the misery of my life. He strewed it at the outset with pleasures mingled with pains; and in the end he has left it to tears, sorrow, and regret.

" I was born in Media, and I can number a long train of illustrious ancestors. My father gained many victories at the head of the Median armies. I lost him in my infancy, and those who had the care of my education taught me to consider his virtues as my most valuable inheritance.

" At the age of fifteen they fixed my establishment. They did not allow me that prodigious number of wives with which in Media people of my birth are usually oppressed : they wished to follow nature, and to teach me that, if the wants of the senses are bounded, those of the heart are still more so.

" Ardasira was not more distinguished from my other wives by her birth than by my love. Her pride was mingled with something so tender, her sentiments were so noble, so different from those which perpetual sub-mission dictates to the women of Asia, her beauty moreover was so great that my eyes could gaze on none but her, and my heart was a stranger to every other.

" Her countenance was heavenly ; her shape, her air, her gracefulness, the sound of her voice, the charm of her discourse all conspired to enchant me. I longed to hear her speak for ever, and I was never tired of beholding her. To me there was nothing so perfect in nature as herself; my imagination could picture nothing which I did not find her possessed of ; and, when I contemplated the happiness of which mortals are susceptible, I always thought of my own.

" My birth, my wealth, my age, and some personal advantages, determined the king to offer me his daughter in marriage. It is an inviolable custom among the Medes that those who receive this honour must send all their other wives away. I saw nothing in this grand alliance but the loss of what was most dear to me in the world : but I was obliged to devour my tears, and to counterfeit gaiety. While all the Court congratulated me on a favour which is there coveted as the highest, Ardasira never asked to see me, and I both dreaded her presence and desired it. I entered her apartment overwhelmed with grief. 'Ardasira,' said I, 'I am about to lose you.' But without either caresses or reproaches, without lifting her eyes or dropping a tear, she remained silent. A deadly paleness overspread her lovely countenance, which expressed a sort of indignation mingled with despair.

" I would have embraced her, but she seemed averse to it ; and she gave no other sign of emotion save an endeavour to escape from my arms.

" It was not the fear of death that made me accept the hand of the princess ; and had I not trembled for Ardasira, I should undoubtedly have exposed myself to the most dreadful vengeance. But when I considered that her death would be the certain consequence of my refusal, my mind was distracted, and I abandoned myself to my fate.

" I was conducted to the royal palace, which I was not again permitted to leave. I beheld that place, made for the humiliation of many and the gratification of one only; that place where, notwithstanding its silence, the sighs of love are scarcely heard; that place in which melancholy and magnificence hold their court; where everything inanimate is gay, and everything that possesses life is sorrowful; where all move, and smile, or are sad at the master's nod.

" I was immediately introduced to the princess, who could survey me with freedom, whilst my looks were fixed on the ground. Strange effects of grandeur! If her eyes were expressive, mine were not permitted to answer. Two eunuchs were in attendance, each armed with a poniard, that I might expiate with my blood the presumption of a look.

" How hard was the trial for a heart like mine! to retire to my chamber a slave of the Court; to live subject to caprice and proud disdain; to feel nothing but a sentiment of awe, and to lose for ever what can compensate even for servitude, the pleasure of loving and being loved!

" But what was my situation when a eunuch from the princess came to make me sign an order for the removal of all my wives from my palace! ' Sign,' said he, ' and acknowledge the benignity of this order. I will report to the princess your readiness to obey.'

" My face was covered with tears; I began to write,

I hesitated—' For Heaven's sake,' said I to the eunuch, ' have a moment's patience—I shall die.'

" ' My lord,' said he, ' your head and mine are at stake; sign—we are already becoming guilty—the moments are counted; I should now be on my way back.'

" My trembling or hasty hand (for my mind was unconscious of its proceedings) traced the most fatal characters it was in its power to form.

" My wives were carried away on the eve of my marriage; but Ardasira, who had gained over one of my eunuchs, dressed in her clothes and veil a slave of her own shape, and concealed herself in a secret place. She had made the eunuch believe that she meant to retire among the priestesses of the gods.

"Ardasira's spirit was too high to conceive that an edict, which without any reason deprived a lawful wife of her rank, could be made for her. She was incapable of respecting power that was abused. She appealed from this tyranny to nature, and from her impotence to her despair.

" The marriage ceremony was performed in the palace. I carried the princess to my own house. There music, dancing, feasting, and everything around us, seemed to express a joy which my heart was far from feeling.

" At the approach of night all the courtiers left us. The eunuchs conducted the princess to her apartment: alas! it was the same in which I had so often sworn eternal fidelity to Ardasira. I retired to mine, full of rage and despair.

" The moment fixed for my approach to the princess

arrived. I entered a vault, unknown even to my servants, through which love had often led me. I was proceeding in the dark, alone, pensive and melancholy, when on a sudden there appeared a light. Ardasira, with a dagger in her hand, stood before me. 'Arsaces,' said she, 'go and tell your new spouse that I am dead : tell her that I have disputed your heart to the last sigh.'

" She was about to strike herself, when I withheld her hand. 'Ardasira,' I cried, 'what a terrible spectacle are you about to present to me!' Then extending my arms, 'Begin rather,' said I, 'by striking him who first yielded to a barbarous law.'

" She turned pale, and the dagger dropped from her hands. I embraced her, and, I know not by what charm, my soul began to grow calm. I held this dear object in my arms, and gave myself up to the pleasure of loving. Every painful idea, even that of my marriage, was obliterated. I thought myself possessed of Ardasira never more to be separated. Strange effect of love! my heart warmed, and my soul became tranquil.

" The words of Ardasira recalled me to myself. 'Arsaces,' said she, 'let us fly, let us quit this unfortunate place. What should we fear? We can love, and we can die.'

" ' Ardasira,' said I, 'I swear that you shall ever be mine ; mine, as if you had never been torn from these arms. I will never more leave you. I call the gods to witness that it is to you alone that I shall owe the happiness of my life. You have proposed a generous enterprise—Love had already suggested it to me : he

L

now again inspires me with it through you; and you shall judge whether I really love you.'

" I left her, and full of impatience and love, I went to give the necessary orders. The door of the princess's chamber was shut. I took with me what gold and jewels I had at hand. I bade my slaves take different roads, and departed alone with Ardasira in the dead of night; full of hopes and full of fears; sometimes losing my natural courage; a prey to every passion, even to remorse, and not knowing whether I were following the path of duty, or that of love, which so often leads one astray.

" I will not detain you with the particulars of the many dangers we encountered. Ardasira, in spite of the weakness of her sex, encouraged me; and though almost dead with fatigue, she continued to follow me. I shunned the society of man, for all men had now become my enemies, and I sought the deserts. I at last arrived among some mountains where only lions and tigers dwell. The presence of these animals tranquillized me.

" ' It is not in these inhospitable regions,' said I to Ardasira, 'that the eunuchs of the princess, or the guards of the King of Media, will seek us.'

" But the wild beasts so thronged around us that I began to be alarmed. I killed with my arrows such of them as approached too near; for instead of encumbering myself with the necessaries of life, I had stored myself with weapons that might procure them. Harassed on all sides, I struck fire with flints, and kindled some dry wood. I passed the night beside these fires, and made a noise with my weapons. Sometimes I set fire to the woods and drove the terrified animals before me. We at last entered a more open country, and admired the deep peace of nature. It suggested to our imagination the time when the gods were born; when beauty first appeared, first felt the genial warmth of love, and when all things first sprung into life.

"At length we passed the confines of Media. It was in the cottage of a shepherd that I fancied myself master of the world; that I was at last able to say that Ardasira was mine, and that I was wholly hers.

"We arrived in Margiana, where our slaves rejoined us. There we lived a pastoral life, far from the world and its bustle. Charmed with each other, we enjoyed our present pleasures, and reflected on our past pains.

"Ardasira related to me what had been her feelings during the time of our separation; her jealousy, when she believed I no longer loved her; her grief, when she knew that I loved her still; her execration of a barbarous law, and her resentment at my submitting to it. She had at first conceived the design of making the princess a victim of her revenge, but soon rejected the idea. She would have been happy in dying before my eyes, for she knew I should be greatly moved. When I held her in my arms, and she proposed to me to quit my native country, then, said she, she had felt sure of me.

"Ardasira had never been so happy: she was enchanted. We did not live amid the splendour of Media; but our manner of life was more delightful. Every thing we had lost enabled her to realise the great sacrifice I had made for her. She now wholly enjoyed

me. In seraglios, those destined abodes of pleasure,
the idea of a rival is ever present ; and although a tender
fair one may enjoy the society of the man she loves,
yet, the stronger her affection, the more is it chequered
with alarm.

" But Ardasira now had no distrust ; our hearts were
knit together. And surely a love like this impresses an
air of gaiety on everything around ; when one object
enchants us, all nature appears cheerful and engaging.
A love like ours resembles that happy infancy to which
everything affords novelty, playfulness, and pleasure.

" I feel a gentle transport whilst I speak to you of
that happy period. Sometimes I lost Ardasira in the
woods, and found her again by the sweet accents of
her voice. She decked herself with flowers which I
gathered, and I adorned myself with those which had
been culled by her hand. The song of the birds, the
murmuring of the fountains, the music and the dancing
of our young slaves, the softness impressed on everything around us, were continual testimonies of the
happiness we enjoyed.

" Sometimes Ardasira dressed herself like a shepherdess, without ornaments or jewels, and appeared in
the charms of native simplicity. At other times she
presented herself richly adorned, and such as she had
appeared when I was first captivated with her beauty
in my Median harem.

" Ardasira employed her women in delightful occupations. They spun the wool of Hircania, and stained
it with the purple of Tyre. And unmingled joy glowed
in every bosom. We descended with pleasure to the

equality of nature: we ourselves were happy, and wished to make all around us happy. False pleasures make men haughty and severe, and such pleasures are always selfish. But true happiness inspires gentleness and benevolence, and diffuses its influence on every hand.

"I remember that Ardasira married one of her favourite maids to a slave of mine whom I had freed. Love and youth had formed this union. The favourite said to Ardasira, 'This is also the first day of your marriage.'

"'Every day of my life,' replied she, 'will be that first day.'

"You will no doubt be surprised that, exiled from Media and proscribed, having had but a moment to prepare for my departure, carrying with me only the money and jewels that were at hand, I should possess sufficient wealth in Margiana to build a palace there, to keep a great number of domestics, and enjoy all the conveniences of life. I was surprised at it myself, and am so still. By a fatality which I cannot explain I thought myself without resources, and yet found them everywhere. Gold, and jewels, and precious stones, seemed to offer themselves to me spontaneously. It was chance or accident, you will say. But circumstances so reiterated and so similar could hardly be the result of mere chance. Ardasira at first thought that I wished to surprise her, and that I had brought wealth with me of which she was ignorant. I believed, in my turn, that she likewise had riches concealed from me. But we were both soon convinced of our mistake. In

my chamber I often found packets containing hundreds
of darics; and Ardasira found boxes full of jewels in
hers. One day, as I was walking in my garden, a little
coffer full of gold pieces appeared in my way, and I
observed another in the hollow trunk of an oak under
which I used to repose. I omit the rest. I was sure
that no one in Media knew the place of my retreat, and
I was as certain that I had no assistance to expect from
that quarter. I tortured my imagination to discover
whence this succour came; but all my conjectures
were in vain."

"People tell wonderful stories," said Aspar, interrupting Arsaces, "of certain powerful genii who attach
themselves to men, and who delight in doing them
good. Nothing I ever heard of this kind before made
the least impression on my mind, but what you tell me
astonishes me. You speak from experience, not from
hearsay."

"Whether this succour," continued Arsaces, "came
by human or supernatural means, it is certain that it
never failed me ; and just as there are many people who
meet with misery wherever they turn, so I found riches
wherever I went. But what is still more surprising,
they always came at the most seasonable moment. I
never saw my treasures near a close but they were
immediately replaced, so attentive was the fate that
watched over us. Nor is this all ; it was not merely our
wants that were provided for, but often our very wishes
were granted. However, I am not fond of dilating on
the marvellous," added he, "and will not detain you
further with particulars which, although I know them

to be true, you will not perhaps find yourself disposed to believe.

" On the eve of our favourite's marriage, a youth as beautiful as love brought me a basket of choice fruit. I gave him a few pieces of silver, which he took, and, leaving his basket, disappeared. I carried the basket to Ardasira, and was surprised to find it so heavy; but when we had eaten the fruit, we found the bottom full of darics. ' It is the genie,' cried everyone, ' who has brought a treasure to defray the expenses of the marriage.'

" ' I am convinced,' said Ardasira, ' that it is a genie who performs these wonders in our favour. Nothing can be more pleasing to superior intelligences than to see those whom they favour love one another; love alone is endowed with perfections which can elevate the human mind to a resemblance with that of the deity. Arsaces, it is a genie who knows my heart, and realises the ardour of my love. Would that I could see him, and that he would tell me the extent of your affection !'

" But I proceed :—Ardasira's passion and mine bore the marks of our different education and of our different characters. Ardasira lived only for love; her passion was her existence; her whole soul was love. It was not possible for her to love me less, nor could she love me more. As for me, my love seemed to be more violent, because it was sometimes interrupted. Ardasira alone was capable of satisfying my passion; but there were circumstances that drew me from it; I often followed the stags in the forest, and went forth to combat the wild beasts.

" I began at last to imagine that the life I led was too obscure. ' I am living,' said I, ' in the dominions of the King of Margiana, why do I not appear at Court?' The glory of my father rushed upon my mind. It is difficult to bear the weight of a great name, for then the virtues of ordinary men are not the goal which we should attain, but the point whence we must start. We are always more eager to fulfil the expectations of others than our own resolves. When I was in Media, I was obliged to humble myself, and to conceal my virtues with more anxiety than my vices. If I was not the slave of the Court, I was the slave of its jealousy. ' But now that I am master of myself,' thought I, ' independent, since I am bound to no country, and as free in the midst of these forests as the lions that inhabit them, my mind will degenerate to the common level, if I continue to tread in the common road.'

" I grew accustomed to these ideas by degrees. Discontent seems so congenial to our nature, that, were we ever so happy, we should still wish to be more so. There is a sort of impatience which attends felicity itself: for as our mind is but a series of ideas, so our heart is but a series of desires. When we find that our happiness cannot be increased, we endeavour to give it a new form. My ambition was sometimes stimulated even by my love. I hoped to become more worthy of Ardasira, and in spite of all her prayers, in spite of all her tears, I left her.

" I will not describe to you the dreadful violence I offered myself; I was a hundred times upon the point of returning, and of throwing myself at Ardasira's feet ;

but the shame of appearing irresolute, the certainty that I should not be able to force myself from her again, the habit I had acquired of imposing obedience upon my heart, even in the most difficult affairs, all determined me to continue my journey.

" I was received by the king with every mark of distinction. I had hardly an opportunity of considering myself a stranger. I made one in all his parties of pleasure ; he preferred me to all others of my age, and there was neither rank nor dignity in Margiana to which I might not have aspired.

" I soon had an opportunity of justifying this favourable opinion of me. The Court of Margiana had long enjoyed a profound peace, but information was received that a vast multitude of barbarians had appeared on the frontiers, that they had decimated the army which had been sent to oppose them, and were advancing by forced marches on the capital. Had the city already been taken by assault, the Court could not have been thrown into greater consternation. The people had never known anything but prosperity. They could not distinguish the degrees of misfortune, nor what can be retrieved from what is irretrievable. They hastily summoned a council, and as I was then with the king, I attended it. The monarch was distracted, and his counsellors also seemed to have lost their reason. It was evidently impossible to save them, except by rousing their courage. The prime minister first gave his opinion ; he proposed to send the king to a place of safety, and then to deliver up the keys of the city to the general of the enemy. He proceeded to state his

M

reasons, and all the council were about to agree with him, when I rose up and interrupted him.

"'If you utter another word,' said I, 'that word shall be your last. A magnanimous prince, and all these brave men, must not waste such precious time in listening to your dastardly counsels.' Then turning to the king: 'A powerful state, sire, does not fall at one blow; you possess a multitude of resources; and although you even had not one left, would you deliberate with this man as to whether you ought to die or follow disgraceful advice? My friends, I swear with you that we will defend the king to our last breath. Let him lead us on, let us arm the people, and let us inspire them with the courage by which we are animated.'

"The city was placed in a state of defence; and I seized upon an outpost with a band of chosen men, composed partly of natives and partly of my own brave followers. We defeated several parties of the enemy. A body of cavalry intercepted their supplies. They had no engines for besieging the city. Our army increased daily. The enemy retired, and Margiana was delivered.

"Amid the noise and tumult of this Court I tasted but false joys. Wherever I turned my eyes Ardasira was wanting, and my heart was constantly yearning for her. I had experienced happiness, and had fled from it; I had quitted real pleasure in pursuit of delusive enjoyments.

"Since my departure Ardasira had been tortured by conflicting passions. They had all seized her in turn, but none of them could satisfy her. She wished to be silent, and she wished to complain; she took up the pen to write to me; indignation made her throw it away. She could not bring herself to express any signs of sensibility, still less could she affect those of indifference. But at last her grief of heart determined her, and she wrote to me the following letter:

" 'Had your heart retained the smallest sentiment of pity, you could never have abandoned me; you would have returned so tender a love; you would have respected our misfortunes; you would have sacrificed to me the vain ideas that seduced you. Cruel man! you would have thought it something to lose a heart that burns only for you. How could you know, whether, seeing you no longer, I should have enough fortitude to endure life? and if I die, barbarous man! can you doubt but that you will be the cause of my death? O gods! you! Arsaces! My love, so ingenious in tormenting me, never before made me dread a punishment like this. I thought I should never weep but for your misfortunes, and that I should remain all my life regardless of my own.'

" I could not read this letter without shedding tears. Grief took possession of my heart; and besides the sentiment of pity, I felt a cruel pang of remorse at having caused the unhappiness of her whom I loved more than life itself.

" At first I conceived the idea of requesting Ardasira to come to Court; but I dwelt on this idea barely a moment. The Court of Margiana is almost the only one in Asia in which the women are not secluded from intercourse with the men. The king was young, and powerful; I reflected that he might do anything, I reflected that he might love, that he might be pleased with Ardasira; and this idea was more dreadful to me than a thousand deaths.

" I had no other course left me but to return to her; and you will be surprised when you know what prevented my doing so. I every moment expected the most splendid marks of gratitude from the king, and I flattered myself that, appearing before Ardasira with new honours, I might the more easily justify myself to her. I thought that she would love me the more, and I anticipated the pleasure of laying my new fortune at her feet.

" I informed her of the reason that made me postpone my departure, and it was this very reason that overwhelmed her with despair. My favour with the king had been so sudden, that it was attributed to a passion which the princess his sister had conceived for me. This is one of those things which are instantly believed when they have once been told. A slave whom Ardasira had sent to attend me wrote to her what he had heard reported. The idea of a rival was death to her; but it was still worse when she heard of the exploits I had performed. She did not doubt but that so much glory would prove an additional incentive to love. ' I am not a princess,' said she in her indignation; ' but I feel that there is not a princess on earth to whom I ought to yield a heart which is mine by right; and if I made him sensible of this in Media I will also make him sensible of it in Margiana.'

" After forming a thousand schemes she at last fixed upon the following one: She dismissed the greater part of her slaves and hired others; she caused a palace to be furnished in the country of the Sogdians, disguised herself, took along with her some eunuchs who were unknown to me, and came secretly to Court. She conversed with the slave who was in her interest, and took measures with him for carrying me off the next day. As I was going to bathe in the river, the slave led me to a place on the shore where Ardasira was waiting. I had no sooner undressed than I was seized, a woman's robe was thrown over me, and I was forced into a closed litter. We travelled day and night, soon passed the boundaries of Margiana, and arrived in the country of the Sogdians. I was shut up in a vast palace, and informed that the princess, who they said had conceived a passion for me, had caused me to be carried off, and conducted secretly to an estate which formed part of her dower.

"Ardasira did not choose to discover herself, nor did she wish that I should be known. She was desirous of deriving enjoyment from my error. All who were not in the secret took her for the princess; and as the fact of a man being shut up in her palace might have cast a slur upon her character, I was allowed to retain my female garments, and was supposed to be a newly-purchased girl destined for her service.

" I was then in the seventeenth year * of my age.

* Persons unacquainted with Eastern history may consider it an error on Montesquieu's part to have made his hero so young. In the East, however, Nature, fostered by the warmth of the climate, shoots up with amazing celerity; and the records of Hindostan inform us that the sons of Shah Jehan, one of the Mogul sovereigns, commanded armies at twelve years of age.

The people around me said that I had all the freshness of youth, and my beauty was extolled as if I had been the daughter of a king.

" Ardasira, who knew that a passion for glory had induced me to quit her, resolved to employ every method to enervate my courage, I was committed to the charge of two eunuchs, who spent whole days in adorning me. They were careful of my complexion, they often led me to the bath, and perfumed me with the most delicate essences. I never went abroad; I was told to work in adorning my own dress; but above all, they endeavoured to inspire me with that obedient spirit to which women are accustomed in the harems of the East.

" I was enraged at seeing myself thus treated. I would have done anything to break my chains; but finding myself without arms, surrounded by people who were continually on the watch, I was afraid not of making, but of failing in my attempt. I hoped that in time I should be less carefully guarded, that I might corrupt some slave, and thus escape from this prison or perish.

" I will confess it; curiosity as to the outcome of all this seemed to quiet my thoughts. In the midst of my shame, grief, and confusion, too, I was surprised to find myself so little inclined to exertion. My thoughts were employed in scheming vast projects, which ended in a slight uneasiness; a secret charm, a power, for which I could not account, detained me in this palace.

" The pretended princess was constantly veiled, and I never heard her voice. She passed almost the whole day in observing me through a grating that was made in my chamber. Sometimes she caused me to be brought to her apartments. There her women sang the most affecting airs, and I thought that they were all expressive of her love. I could never be too near her, she occupied herself only with me; there was always something in my dress that she thought could be improved; she would unfasten my hair and dress it again, and she was never content with what she had done.

"One day I was told that she permitted me to wait upon her. I found her reclining on a purple sofa, and still covered with her veil; her head was gently inclined, her attitude, softly pensive and languishing. As I approached, one of her women thus addressed me: 'You are the favourite of Love; it is he who under this disguise has brought you hither. The princess loves you. She is made to subdue every heart, but 'tis yours alone that she desires.'

"'How,' said I, sighing, 'how can I give a heart that is not mine? My beloved Ardasira possesses it wholly, and it shall be hers for ever.'

"I could not observe what emotion these words produced in Ardasira, but she has since told me, that she never experienced so much joy.

"'Rash man,' said her attendant, 'the princess, like the gods when we are so unfortunate as not to adore them, cannot but be offended at such language.'

"'I will pay her,' I replied, 'every kind of homage; my respect, my gratitude, shall never cease. But destiny, rigorous destiny, does not permit me to love her. Great princess,' added I, throwing myself at her

feet, ' I conjure you by your glory to forget a man whose
heart, being eternally devoted to another, can never be
worthy of yours.'

" I heard her heave a deep sigh, and I thought I
saw her face covered with tears. I upbraided myself
for my insensibility ; I wished something impossible—
to continue faithful to my own passion without driving
her to despair.

" I was at last led back to my apartment, and a few
days afterwards I received the following missive in a
handwriting which was unknown to me :—

" ' The princess's love is violent, but not tyrannical ;
she will not even complain of your refusal, if you con-
vince her that it is justifiable. Come then, and inform
her of the reasons you have to be so faithful to that
Ardasira.'

" I was again conducted into her presence. I related
to her the whole history of my life, and, whilst I spoke
to her of my love, I heard her sigh. She held my hand
in hers, and, during those affecting moments, she often
pressed it with involuntary force.

" ' Begin again,' suddenly said one of her women, ' at
the part where you were so afflicted, when the King of
Media gave you his daughter in marriage. Tell us
again about your fears for Ardasira during your flight.
Describe again to the princess what pleasures you
enjoyed in your Margian solitude.'

" I had not told her every circumstance. So I began
again, and she listened as if she heard me for the first
time. At last I concluded, and she looked as if she
wished that I had been about to begin the narrative.

" On the ensuing day, the following letter was sent to me : ' I am convinced of your love, and do not desire that you should sacrifice it to me. But are you sure that this Ardasira still loves you ? Perhaps it is for an ungrateful woman that you refuse the heart of a princess who adores you.'

" I returned this answer: ' Ardasira loves me with so much passion, that it would be vain to pray the gods to increase her love. Alas! perhaps she has loved me too much. I remember a letter that she wrote to me some time after I had left her. Had you read the terrible, the tender expressions of her love, you would have been affected by them. I am afraid that, whilst I am confined here, her grief at having lost me, and her disgust with life, may have caused her to take a resolution of a nature to bring me to the grave.'

" I received this reply : ' Be happy, Arsaces ; and may your heart remain with the woman you love ; as for myself, I only ask your friendship.'

" The next day I was again admitted to the princess's apartment, where everything seemed calculated to awaken voluptuous desires ; the atmosphere was laden with the most delightful perfumes ; the princess was reclining languishingly upon a bed hung round with garlands of flowers. She held out her hand, and made me sit down beside her. Grace appeared in everything around and about her, even in the veil that concealed her features ! I could discern the elegance of her form through the close thin vestment she wore, which alternately hid and displayed the most ravishing beauties. She saw that my eyes were

N

engaged, and when she observed them grow some-
what inflamed, she allowed her robe to fall slightly,
and I beheld her shoulders which were of transcendant
beauty. At that instant she pressed my hand; whilst
my eyes wandered over her lovely figure. 'None,' I
exclaimed, 'but my dear Ardasira, can be so beautiful ;
and I call the gods to witness that my fidelity—'

" At that moment she threw herself upon my neck,
and locked me in her arms. The chamber was immediately darkened, her veil fell off, and she kissed me.
I was enraptured. A sudden flame ran through all
my veins, and fired all my senses. The idea of
Ardasira was gone. A faint recollection—it appeared
but as a dream—occurred to my mind as I was about
—about to prefer her to herself. Eagerly did I press
her to my throbbing heart. Her divine, her matchless
beauty had fairly intoxicated me. Love, at that
moment, made himself known but by his fury. He
was hurrying on to victory; but Ardasira suddenly
released herself from my embrace, several of her
attendants entered the apartment, she hastily fled
from me, and disappeared.

" I returned to my apartments, astonished at my
inconstancy. The next day the habit of my sex was
restored to me, and in the evening I was conducted to
her the idea of whom still continued to enchant me.
I approached her, threw myself on my knees, and,
transported with desire, talked to her of my passion,
reproached myself for my refusals, prayed, promised,
demanded, ventured to say and seemed about to attempt
everything. But I found a curious change in her; she

appeared quite cold; and when she had sufficiently discouraged me, and had entertained herself with my embarrassment, she spoke to me, and thus it was that for the first time I heard her voice: 'Do you not desire,' said she, 'to see the face of her you love?'

"The sound of her voice struck me, and I stood motionless. I hoped that it was Ardasira's, and I dreaded to find my hope realised.

"'Remove this veil,' said she.

"I did so, and indeed beheld the countenance of Ardasira. I would have spoken, but could not. Love, surprise, joy, shame, every passion seized me in turn.

"'You are Ardasira!' said I.

"'Yes, perfidious man,' she answered, 'I am.'

"'Ardasira,' said I, in broken accents, 'why thus trifle with an unhappy passion?' As I spoke I would have embraced her.

"'My lord,' said she, 'I am yours. But alas! I hoped to find you more faithful. Be satisfied with reigning here. Punish me, if you think proper, for what I have done—Ah! Arsaces,' she added, with a tear, 'you did not deserve it.'

"'My beloved Ardasira,' I replied, 'why drive me to despair? Would you have me insensible to charms that I have always adored? You must allow that you are not very consistent with yourself. Was it not yourself that I was charmed with? Are not these the beauties that have always enchanted me?'

"'Ah!' said she, 'you would have loved them in another.'

"'I could not have loved any other but you. What-

ever was not you, would have disgusted me. How
disappointed I should have been if I had not seen that
beautiful face, heard that sweet voice, or beheld those
eyes? But for heaven's sake, do not drive me to
despair. Consider, that of all the infidelities that I
have been guilty of, this is undoubtedly the most
pardonable.'

" I perceived by the soft languor of her eyes that she
was no longer angry ; I knew it also by the faintness
of her voice. I held her in my arms. Oh ! the happiness of embracing the dear object of our love, after a
long and tedious absence ! How shall I express the
transports which only true lovers can feel, when our
passion increases from itself; when we mutually
promise, and demand, and obey, when we feel that we
possess all, and yet think that we have not enough ;
when the soul is lost in itself, and seems as though
it would grasp at joys beyond the very powers of
nature!

" Ardasira, recovering her self-possession, at last said
to me : ' My dear Arsaces, my love for you has made
me follow a very extraordinary course ; but extreme
love regards neither law nor moderation. They know
it little who do not number its caprices among its
greatest pleasures. In the name of the gods I conjure
you never to leave me again. What can you want?
If you love me, you are happy. And you may be sure
that no mortal was ever so much beloved as yourself.
Say, promise, swear to me, that you will never more
forsake me.'

" I swore it a thousand and a thousand times ; my

oaths were only interrupted by my caresses, and she believed them.

"How rapturous is love even after the violence of its transports; when, after having appealed to the senses, it addresses itself to the mind; when, after having feasted upon beauty, it delights in contemplating the graces!

"We lived in Sogdiana in unspeakable felicity. I had remained but a few months at the Court of Margiana, and that short sojourn had cured me of ambition. I had enjoyed the favour of the king, but I had soon perceived that he could not forgive me for my courage and his terror. My presence there embarassed him, and it was indeed impossible that he could love me. His courtiers perceived it, and were on their guard not to overrate my merit. In order that the honour of saving the state from danger might not be attributed to me, it was universally allowed at Court that the state had never been in danger.

"Thus, equally disgusted with slavery and slaves, I cherished no other passion but my love for Ardasira; and I thought myself a hundred times happier in remaining in the dependence of the woman I fondly loved, than in submitting to that of another whom I could but hate.

"The good genie seemed to have followed us. We found ourselves in the enjoyment of the same abundance, and daily witnessed new prodigies.

"A fisherman came to sell us a fish; and a rich ring was brought to me which had been found in its mouth. One day, as I was in want of money, I sent a few jewels to be sold at the nearest town: the price of them

was brought to me, and a few days afterwards I found
the jewels themselves on my table.

"'Great gods!' cried I, 'is it then impossible for me
to grow poor?'

"We wished to try the genie, and we asked a very
large sum of him. He soon made us acknowledge that
our wishes had been unreasonable. A few days afterwards we found upon our table the smallest sum we
had ever received. We could hardly refrain from
laughing at the sight of it.

"'The genie sports with us,' said Ardasira.

"'Ah!' cried I, 'the gods are excellent dispensers;
the mediocrity they grant us is far preferable to the
treasures which they deny us.'

"We were not haunted by any of the malignant
passions. Blind ambition, the thirst of wealth, the
desire of dominion—all were strangers to us, and
seemed the passions of another world. Such enjoyments are only made to fill the void that exists in souls
which nature has left empty. They have been invented
by imaginations incapable of conceiving better feelings.

"I have told you that we were adored by the little
family that formed our household. Ardasira and I
loved each other, and happiness is the natural effect of
love. But that general affection which some people win
from those around them is capable of inspiring even
greater happiness than love itself can bring. A good heart
cannot fail to experience exquisite delight upon being
the object of general affection. How admirable is this
law of nature! Man is never less selfish than when he
appears to be most so. The heart is never the heart

but when it diffuses itself, for its pleasures come from
without. Hence it is that those ideas of grandeur,
which always contract the heart, deceive such as are
intoxicated with them; hence their astonishment at
finding themselves unhappy in the enjoyment of possessions with which they had promised themselves felicity.
Not finding it, they think that they have not attained
to a sufficient degree of wealth or greatness; and there-
fore they pursue their ambitious course still further.
If they do not succeed, their misery is increased, and even
if they do, they still fail to attain complete happiness.

"It is pride which, by taking possession of us,
prevents us from remaining in possession of our own
minds: and which, by making all our desires centre in
ourselves, never fails to bring melancholy in its train.
This melancholy proceeds from the loneliness of the
heart, which is made for enjoyment, but under these
circumstances never feels it, and for benevolence, but
when thus situated is ever selfish.

"Thus we might have tasted those pleasures which
nature never fails to bestow on those who do not shun
her; we might have spent our days in joy, in innocence,
and peace; we might have counted our years by the
renewal of the flowers and of the fruits; we might have
forgotten the number of them in the rapidity of a
happy life; I might have seen Ardasira every day,
and every day have told her how I loved her; the same
earth might at last have received us both. But alas!
my happiness vanished in an instant, and I experienced,
the most dreadful reverse.

"The prince of the country was a tyrant capable of

every crime: but nothing rendered him so odious as
the continual outrages he offered to a sex whom we are
hardly permitted to assault even with our eyes.   He
had learnt from a female slave, who had quitted the
seraglio of Ardasira, that she was the most beautiful
woman of the East.   This sufficed to determine him to
tear her from my arms.   One night a large body of
armed men surrounded my house, and in the morning I
received an order from the tyrant to send Ardasira to him.
I saw the impossibility of saving her.   My first idea
was to kill her as she lay asleep.   I seized my sword, I
ran, entered her chamber and drew aside the curtains;
but then I suddenly started back with horror, and my
blood ran cold.   A new frenzy seized me; I thought
of throwing myself upon the guards, and of slaying
all who opposed me.   But at last a less rash design
presented itself to my mind.   I resolved to resume the
dress I had worn a few months before; and under the
name of Ardasira, to enter the litter destined for her,
and allow myself to be carried to the tyrant.   I could
devise no other resource, and besides, I felt a secret
pleasure in performing a courageous action in the garb
which blind love had formerly utilized to debase, as
it were, my sex.

" I executed this plan with composure.   I gave orders
that the danger I ran should be concealed from Ardasira,
and that as soon as I departed my slaves should convey
her to another country.   I took a slave along with me
whose courage I had previously tried, and delivered
myself up to the women and eunuchs whom the tyrant
had sent.   We were not two days upon the road, and

it was night when I arrived. The tyrant was celebrating a feast with his women and his courtiers in a garden pavilion. He was in that state of stupid gaiety which is the result of debauchery carried to excess. He commanded that I should be brought into his presence; I entered the festal hall; he made me sit down beside him, and I had fortitude enough to conceal my rage and the disorder of my soul. I was, however, irresolute. I wished to attract the notice of the tyrant, and when he turned his eyes upon me I felt my fury redoubled.

"'Because he thinks that I am Ardasira,' said I to myself, 'he dares to love me.'

"Then I imagined that my injuries were multiplied, and that he had found a thousand ways of outraging my love. I was, however, about to enjoy the most dreadful vengeance. He began to grow inflamed, and I beheld him insensibly approaching to his destruction. He left the hall, and led me to a distant apartment in the garden, accompanied only by an eunuch and my slave. He was about to become acquainted with my sex.

"'This steel,' cried I, 'will show you that I am a man. Die! and may it be told in hell that the husband of Ardasira has punished your crimes!'

"He fell at my feet, and the door of the apartment was immediately opened, for as soon as my slave had heard my voice, he had killed the eunuch who guarded the portal, and entered. We fled, but wandered for some time in the gardens, till we met a man whom I seized.

"'I will plunge this dagger into your heart,' said I, 'if you do not instantly show me the way out of this place.'

o

" He was a gardener, and, trembling with fear, he led me to a gate which he opened; I made him.shut it behind us, and ordered him to follow me. I changed my clothes, and assumed the habit of a slave. We wandered in the woods, and by an unhoped-for chance, when we were overcome with fatigue, we found a merchant whose camels were feeding, and we compelled him to conduct us out of this fatal country.

" In proportion as the dangers to which I was exposed diminished, my mind became less at ease. I had to find Ardasira, and I was all alarm for her safety. Her women and eunuchs had concealed from her the horror of our situation; but not finding me with her, she had concluded me guilty; and was convinced that I had broken the innumerable oaths of fidelity I had sworn to her. She could not conceive a reason for my apparent barbarity in ordering her to be carried away without informing her of my intentions. Love is easily convinced of what it dreads and thus life became insupportable to her: she swallowed poison. However, it did not operate quickly, and when I arrived I found her alive though very weak.

" ' Ardasira,' cried I, ' must I lose you ? you are dying. Cruel Ardasira ! alas, what have I done ? '

" She shed a few tears. ' Arsaces,' said she, ' but a moment ago death appeared delightful to me; now, however, that I see you, how dreadful is its approach ! I feel that I wish to live again for you, and that my soul departs unwillingly. Cherish my memory, and if I learn that it is dear to you, rest assured that I shall not be tormented in the shades below. I have this consolation at least, my dear Arsaces, that I die in your arms.'

"She expired. It is impossible to conceive how it was that I did not die with her. I was torn from her body, and I thought they were tearing me from myself. I fixed my eyes upon her, and remained motionless and insensible. On beholding the melancholy spectacle presented to my sight, I felt my mind regain all its sensibility. But I was dragged away. As I turned my eyes towards the fatal object of my grief, I would have given a thousand lives for another look. I became frantic, I seized my sword, and was about to plunge it into my bosom, but was prevented. I left that fatal palace and never returned there. My reason forsook me; I roamed through the woods, and filled the air with my lamentations. When I became more composed my soul turned irresistibly to my grief. There now seemed nothing in the world for me but sorrow, and the name of Ardasira. That name I uttered in a frantic voice, and then became silent. I resolved to take away my own life, and suddenly grew furious.

"'You would die,' said I to myself, 'whilst Ardasira is unrevenged! You would die, and the son of the tyrant is in Hyrcania, wallowing in pleasure! He lives and you would die!'

"I set out in quest of him. I understood that he had declared war against you, and I flew to join you. I arrived three days before the battle, and performed the action you know of. I might have killed the tyrant's son; but I chose rather to make him my prisoner. I wish that he may drag out in shame and in chains, a

life as miserable as mine.   I hope he will one day learn
that I have cut off the last of his race.   I must own,
however, that, since I have taken this revenge, I do not
find myself any the happier, and I begin to perceive
that the hope of vengeance is more grateful than
vengeance itself.   My fury that I have satisfied, the
action which you witnessed, the acclamations of the
people, even your friendship, my lord, do not restore to
me that which I have lost."

The surprise of Aspar had begun almost with the
narrative to which he had been listening.   The moment
he had heard the name of Arsaces he had recognised the
husband of the queen.   Reasons of state had obliged
him to send Ismenia, the younger daughter of the late
king, into Media, where he had had her educated in
secret, under the name of Ardasira.   He had married
her to Arsaces, he had always retained confidential
servants in their harem ; and he was the genie who, by
the intervention of these servants, had conveyed so
much wealth into Arsaces' abode, and who, by very
simple means, had given rise to their belief in so many
miracles.

Aspar had had very powerful reasons for concealing
Ardasira's parentage from her husband.   Arsaces, who
was so brave, might have asserted the rights of his
wife to the throne of Bactra, and have involved the
kingdom in war.   But these reasons no longer existed,
and as he listened to the story of Arsaces, he was over
and over again upon the point of interrupting him.
However, he considered that it was not yet time to
inform him of his destiny.   A minister, accustomed to

weigh his thoughts, never steps beyond the line of prudence; and the thoughts of Aspar were employed in preparing, not in precipitating, a great event.

Two days afterwards a report was circulated that the eunuch had placed a false Ismenia on the throne. From murmuring, the people proceeded to sedition. They surrounded the palace, and loudly demanded the head of Aspar. The eunuch commanded one of the gates to be opened; and mounted on an elephant, he advanced into the crowd.

"Bactrians," said he, "favour me with your attention." And as they still continued to murmur: "Hear me, I say," cried he; "if you can kill me now, you can equally well take my life a few moments hence. Here is a paper written and sealed by the hand of the late king; prostrate yourselves, and worship, I will read it."

These were its contents: "Heaven has bestowed upon me two daughters, who resemble each other so strongly that all eyes might be deceived. I am afraid that this may give occasion to great troubles and to still more fatal wars. Do you, then, Aspar, the light of the empire, take the younger of the two, send her secretly into Media, and there let her be taken care of. Let her remain there under a feigned name so long as the good of the state shall require it."

Aspar laid this writing on his head, bowed, and resumed his speech: "Ismenia is dead; you cannot doubt it; but her sister, the young Ismenia, sits upon the throne. Is it just on your part to complain because, seeing the death of the queen approaching, I caused her sister to be brought here from the heart of Asia? Can you reproach me for having had the happiness of restoring her to you, and of placing her on a throne which, since the death of her sister, has been hers by right? If I concealed the death of the queen, did not the state of affairs require it? Do you blame me for having performed an act of fidelity, with circumspection and discretion? Lay down your arms, I command you. So far you are not criminals; but from this moment, should you persist, you would become so."

Aspar then explained to them how he had entrusted the young Ismenia to two aged eunuchs, who had transported her to Media under a feigned name; how he had effected her marriage with one of the greatest· lords of that kingdom, and had caused her to be watched over in all the countries to which her fate had led her; how the illness of the queen had determined him to cause the younger Ismenia to be brought to Bactra and kept secretly in the seraglio; and how, after the death of the queen, he had placed her sister on the throne.

As the waves of the agitated ocean are stilled by the zephyrs, so the people grew calm at the words of Aspar. Nothing was heard but acclamations of delight, and all the temples resounded with the name of the young Ismenia.

Aspar incited Ismenia that she might have the curiosity to see the stranger who had rendered such signal service to Bactra; he persuaded her to give him a brilliant audience. It was resolved that the nobles and the people should be assembled, that he should be declared general of the armies of the state, and that the queen should gird him with the sword. The grandees of the kingdom were ranged around a great hall, and a crowd of the people occupied the centre and the entrance. The queen was seated on her throne in magnificent apparel. Her head was crowned with jewels, and according to the custom at those solemnities, her face was unveiled, and the people beheld the countenance of beauty itself. Arsaces appeared, and acclamations resounded. After a moment's silence, with his eyes cast on the ground out of respect, he began to address the queen :—

"Madam," said he, in a low and broken voice, "if anything could restore tranquillity to my soul, and give me comfort under afflictions—"

But the queen did not suffer him to proceed any further; she had thought at first that she recollected his face and she instantly knew his voice. It was that of Arsaces. Transported with joy, and hardly knowing what she did, she sprang from her throne, and threw herself at his feet.

"My afflictions have been greater than yours," cried she, "my dear Arsaces. Alas! I thought that I should never see you more, after the fatal moment that separated us. My grief has been extreme."

Then as though she had passed all at once from one expression of love to another, or as if she was uncertain with regard to the propriety of the impetuous emotion she had just shown, she suddenly arose, and a modest blush overspread her face.

"Bactrians," said she, "it is at the feet of my

husband that you have seen me fall. I am happy that
I have had it in my power to display the sincerity
of my love before you. I descended from my throne
because I sat on it without him; and without him, I
call the gods to witness it, I will not return thither. I
have the pleasure of knowing that the most brilliant
action of my reign has been performed by him, and that
it was for me that he performed it. Nobles, people,
citizens, do you think that he who reigns over me is
worthy of reigning over you? Do you approve of my
choice? Do you elect Arsaces king? Say, speak."

The last words of the queen were hardly pronounced,
when the whole palace resounded with acclamations;
and nothing was heard but the names of Arsaces and
Ismenia.

During all this time, Arsaces seemed lost in amaze-
ment. He would have spoken but could not find the
power of utterance; he would have advanced, but
remained without motion. His senses were fascinated;
he did not see the queen; he did not see the crowd;
he scarcely heard their reiterated acclamations. Joy
had so deranged his faculties that he seemed insensible
even of his felicity.

But when Aspar had dismissed the people, Arsaces
bowed his head over the queen's hand.

"Ardasira, you live; you live, my beloved Ardasira!
I have been dying of grief ever since I lost you. How
have the gods restored you to life?"

He was then hastily informed that one of her women
had substituted an intoxicating liquor for the poison;
that Ardasira had remained for three days without giving

any sign of motion; that when she was restored to life the first word she uttered was the name of Arsaces; that her eyes had opened only to behold him; that she had caused him to be sought for everywhere, and had sought for him anxiously herself; that Aspar had caused her to be brought to Bactra, and, after the death of her sister, had placed her upon the throne.

Aspar had prepared the interview between Arsaces and Ismenia. But he recollected the last sedition. He imagined that, after having taken upon himself to place Ismenia on the throne, it would not be proper for him to seem instrumental in the elevation of Arsaces. It was a maxim with him never to do in person what he could instigate others to do for him, and to love good from whatever quarter it came. Besides, knowing the perfections of character possessed by both Arsaces and Ismenia, he wished to make these perfections appear conspicuously. He wished to obtain for the queen and her husband that respect which great souls always challenge, whenever they have an opportunity of making themselves known.

He wished to procure for them that love which is always bestowed on those who have experienced great misfortunes. He wished to call forth that admiration which ever attends those who are capable of feeling the amiable passions. In short, he thought that nothing but the course he followed was more likely to divest Arsaces of the quality of stranger, and to win him that of Bactrian, in the hearts of all the people of Bactra.

The happiness which Arsaces enjoyed appeared inconceivable to him. Ardasira, whom he had thought

P

dead, was restored to him; Ardasira was Ismenia; Ardasira was Queen of Bactra, and had made him king. The transition was natural from the sentiment of greatness to that of love. He was charmed with the crown which, far from being a mark of independence, incessantly reminded him that it was hers; he loved the throne, because he possessed the hand that had led him to it.

Ismenia enjoyed for the first time the pleasure of perceiving that she was a great queen. Her prosperity had been great before the arrival of Arsaces, but her heart had been incapable of enjoying it; in the midst of her court she had found herself alone; millions of men were at her feet, and yet she thought herself abandoned.

Arsaces immediately ordered the Prince of Hyrcania to be brought before him.

"Now," said he, "I have ordered you to appear in my presence that the chains may drop from your hands. It is not seemly that there should be a single unhappy being in the empire of the happiest of men. Although I have conquered you, I am persuaded that you do not yield to me in courage, but I beg that you will consent to yield to me in generosity."

The queen's disposition was all sweetness and gentleness; such pride as was natural to her, disappearing on all proper occasions:—"Pardon me," said she to the Prince of Hyrcania, "if I did not make the wished-for return to a passion which I knew could not be lawfully gratified. Arsaces' wife could not be yours; if you are disposed to complain, you must complain only of fate. If Hyrcania and Bactra do not form one empire, they

are, however, states destined by nature to be allies.
Ismenia can make offer of friendship, though she could
not promise love."

"I am," replied the prince, "overwhelmed with so
many misfortunes, and overcome with so many favours,
that I know not whether I am an instance of good or
evil fortune. I took up arms against you to revenge an
affront which you had not offered me. You had committed no fault, and I had performed no meritorious
service to induce heaven to favour my enterprise. I
will return to Hyrcania, and there I shall soon forget
my misfortunes; if I do not number among them the
misfortune of having seen you, and that of seeing you
no more. Your beauty will be celebrated in all the
East. It will render this age in which you live more
illustrious than any other; and in future times, the
names of Arsaces and Ismenia will be the most
favourite titles of lovers and their mistresses."

Sometime afterwards an unforeseen circumstance required the presence of Arsaces in a certain province of
the empire: he quitted Ismenia. How tender was her
farewell! how delicious were their tears! It was not
so much a subject of affliction as an occasion of soft
sensations. The grief of parting was cheered by the
thoughts of the pleasure which they would experience
in meeting again.

During the absence of the king everything was so
disposed by his orders, that the time, the place, the
persons, indeed every circumstance presented to Ismenia
some token of his remembrance. He was at a distance,
but his actions spoke him present; all things conspired

to recall his image! Ismenia saw him not, but on every
hand she beheld some proof of his love.

Arsaces wrote continually to Ismenia. In one letter
she read: "I have seen the magnificent cities that
lead to your frontiers; I have seen innumerable people
fall prostrate at my feet. Everything told me that I
reigned in Bactra; but I saw not her who had made
me king, and I felt king no longer."

In another letter he said: "If heaven granted me
the draught of immortality so eagerly sought for in the
East, you should drink in the same cup as myself, or it
should not touch my lips: you should be immortal with
me, or I should die with you."

In another: "I have given your name to the city I
have built; I am convinced that it will be inhabited by
the happiest of your subjects."

In another letter, after saying everything tender and
affectionate which love could dictate respecting the
charms of the queen's person, he added: "I say these
things to you without seeking to flatter you. I wish
to relieve the tediousness of my absence; and I feel that
my soul is gratified by talking of you even to yourself."

At last she received the following letter: "I used
to count the days; I now only count the minutes, and
these minutes are longer than the days. Fair queen!
my soul becomes less and less tranquil the nearer I
approach you."

After the return of Arsaces, embassies arrived from
every quarter, and some of them were of a singular
nature. Arsaces sat on a throne erected in the court
of the palace. The ambassador of Parthia entered first:

he was mounted on a fiery steed, and did not dismount, but spoke thus: " A tiger of Hyrcania desolated the plains ; an elephant trampled him under foot. A young tiger remained, and he was already as cruel as his father ; the elephant, a second time, delivered the country. All the animals that dread the beasts of prey came to feed around him. He was delighted to think that he was their protector, and he said to himself: ' The tiger is called the king of the beasts, but no, he is only their tyrant, 'tis I who am their king.' "

The ambassador of the Persians spoke thus : " At the beginning of time, the moon was married to the sun ; every star in the firmament paid their addresses to her. ' Look at the sun,' said she to them, ' and then look at yourselves; all of you together shed not so much light as he.' "

Next came the ambassador of Egypt, who said : " When Isis espoused the great Osiris, their marriage was the foundation of the prosperity of Egypt, and the mainspring of its fecundity. Such will be the destiny of Bactra ; it will become happy by the marriage of its gods."

Arsaces caused his name and that of Ismenia to be inscribed on the walls of all the palaces. The letters were intermingled and cyphered in every corner. Painters were prohibited from representing Arsaces without Ismenia.

Of all the actions in which severity was requisite he chose to appear as the author ; but every act of grace or favour proceeded in the names of Arsaces and Ismenia conjointly.

"I love you," said he to her, "on account of that celestial beauty and those graces that are ever new; I love you still more, because I know that when I have performed any action worthy of a great king, I am then most approved by you. It was your pleasure to make me your king, when my heart was only engrossed with the happiness of being your husband ; and whenever it has been necessary for my glory you have taught me to forego those pleasures in which we have so rapturously indulged together. You have accustomed my soul to clemency ; and even when you have demanded things which could not be granted, you have always made me respect the heart that demanded them. The women of your palace have not entered into the intrigues of the Court; they have adorned themselves with modesty, and have avoided everything which they should not love. I believe that heaven has designed me for a great prince, since even in those difficulties in which kings are generally conquered, it has enabled me to find assistance to virtue."

Never did Bactra experience happier times. Arsaces and Ismenia were wont to say that they reigned over the best people in the universe ; and the Bactrians declared that they lived under the best of sovereigns.

Arsaces said that, being born a subject, his greatest wish had been to live under the government of a good prince ; and that undoubtedly his subjects formed the same desire. He added that, possessing the heart of Ismenia, it was his duty to win for her the hearts of mankind. He could not bestow a new throne upon her, but he could bring her virtues to adorn her own.

He thought that the memory of his love would descend to posterity, and that it could not descend better than in company with his fame. He wished to have these words inscribed upon his tomb: "The husband of Ismenia was a king who enjoyed the affection of all good men."

He said that he loved Aspar, his prime-minister, because he spoke always of the people, seldom of the king, and never of himself. "Aspar possesses," said Arsaces, "three great qualities; he has a correct judgment, a tender heart, and a benevolent disposition."

Arsaces often spoke of the mildness of his own administration. He said that he was anxious to keep his hands clean; because the first crime he should commit would determine the whole of his future life, and would be the first link in a chain formed of a multitude of other crimes.

"I might punish a man upon suspicion," said he, "and hope that the matter would rest there: but would that be the case? By no means. New suspicions would arise in crowds against the friends and relations of the man I had put to death. These would prove the source of a second crime. These violent actions would make me believe that I must be hated by my subjects: and then I should begin to fear them. Hence occasions for more executions would arise—occasions which would give birth to renewed terrors. If my life were once marked with these stains, the despair of obtaining a virtuous reputation would seize upon me. And as it would be impossible for me to wipe away the guilt of my past crimes, I should grow indifferent about my future conduct."

Arsaces was so anxious to maintain the ancient laws and customs of the Bactrians that he always trembled at the mention of a reform of abuses; for he had often remarked, that people gave the name of law to whatever was agreeable to their own views, whilst whatever ran counter to their interests they called abuses. "In the correction of abuses," he said, "men often destroy what they pretend to reform."

He was convinced that goodness cannot exist in a state except it be conveyed through the channel of the laws; that the only way of establishing permanent prosperity was by doing good as the laws directed; and that the surest way of introducing permanent evil was to commit evil in spite of them.

He was persuaded that the duty of a prince did not so much consist in guarding the laws against the passions of others as against his own; that the general desire of rendering mankind happy was natural to princes; but that this desire became nugatory if princes did not continually endeavour to acquire the knowledge necessary to carry it into effect; that, most fortunately, the great art of governing required judgment rather than genius; a desire to acquire knowledge rather than extensive information; practical skill rather than theoretical proficiency; a certain acuteness in discerning the characters of men, rather than capacity for forming them; that knowledge of mankind is acquired, like everything else, by intercourse with men; that faults and vices can be hidden only with the greatest difficulty; that most men wear a disguise, but that it is generally so loose and ill-fitting that it often leaves some flaw uncovered.

Arsaces never spoke of the affairs which he happened to have with foreign states; but he liked to discourse of those that related to the internal situation of his kingdom, because this was the best means of becoming well acquainted with his possessions: and on these occasions he used to say, that a good prince ought to be discreet, but that he might sometimes carry his reserve to extremes.

He said, he could feel within himself that he was a good king; that he was gentle, affable, and humane; that he was fond of glory, and that he loved his subjects: yet, if with these good qualities he had not stored his mind with the great principles of government, the most grievous misfortune in the world must have befallen his subjects; they would have had a good king, and they might have been sensible of their happiness; and yet that blessing which providence had bestowed on them might have proved, in some measure, useless to them.

"He who expects to find happiness on a throne," said Arsaces, "deceives himself. He can there enjoy only the happiness that he brings with him; and he often risks even the happiness which he thus brings. If the gods then," added he, "have not instituted power for the happiness of those who govern, they must have instituted it for the happiness of those who obey."

Arsaces knew when to give, because he knew how to refuse. "It often happens," said he, "that four villages are not an adequate present for a great lord, who stands

Q

on the brink of ruin ; nor to the man of low birth about to become a great lord. It is easy to enrich poverty of condition ; but it is impossible to enrich the poverty born of luxury."

Arsaces was more inclined to enter the cottages of the peasants than the palaces of the great. " It is there," said he, "that I find my real counsellors. There, also, I am made to remember what my palace has made me forget. The humble tenants lay before me their necessities. Great distress in a state is compounded of the petty misfortunes of individuals. I inform myself of all these misfortunes, which collectively might create my own. It is in these cottages that I become acquainted with those mournful sights which are always objects of delight to those who have it in their power to relieve them, and which tell me that I may yet become a greater prince than I am. There I behold joy succeeding tears, whilst in my own palace I seldom see anything but tears succeeding joy."

He was told one day, that on some occasion of public rejoicing his praises had been celebrated by a company of comedians.

" Do you know," said he, " why I permit such people to praise me ? It is that I may despise flattery, and make it detested by men of worth. My power is so great, that it will always be natural for the selfish to seek to please me. I hope, however, that the gods will never suffer me to feel gratified with flattery. As to you, my friends, always tell me the truth ; it is the only thing in the world that I wish for, because it is the only thing in the world that I am in danger of lacking."

The troubles, that had embittered the close of the reign of Artamenes, proceeded from some small people in the neighbourhood, between Media and Bactra, whom this king had conquered in his youth. They were his allies, but he had wished to make them his subjects. This made them his enemies; and, as they inhabited the mountains, they were never completely subdued. On the contrary, the Medes employed them to excite disturbances in the kingdom. The successes of the conqueror had thus in a great measure weakened the authority of the monarch; and when Arsaces mounted the throne this nation was not yet reconciled to the Bactrian yoke. The intrigues of the Medes soon induced them to revolt. Arsaces flew to the spot and subdued them. Then he summoned the people together and thus addressed them :—

"I know that you only suffer the dominion of the Bactrians with impatience, and this does not surprise me. You loved your ancient kings who loaded you with kindness. It is my duty to act in such a way that by my moderation and my justice you may consider me as the worthy successor of those whom you so highly revere." He then ordered into his presence the two chiefs who had been most active in the revolt, and said to the people: "I have caused these men to be brought before you, that you may judge them yourselves."

Each fancied that he might justify himself by condemning them.

"Acknowledge," said Arsaces, "the happiness you enjoy in living under a king who divests himself of passion when he punishes, and only yields to it when he rewards; who knows that the glory of conquests depends but on chance, and that the glory of forgiveness depends on himself. You shall live happy under my reign, and you shall preserve your customs and your laws. Forget that you are subdued by my arms, I desire that you should only feel subdued by my affection."

The whole nation came to thank Arsaces for his clemency, and for the blessing of peace. Some old men were the orators; and the first of them spoke thus: "Methinks I behold those lofty trees which are the ornament of our country. You are the trunk, and we are the leaves; the leaves shall protect the trunk from the burning influence of the sun."

The second thus addressed him: "You may have asked the gods to level our mountains, that they might not screen us from your arms; now, however, implore them to raise those mountains to the clouds that they may the more effectually defend you from your enemies."

Then the third said: "Survey the river that waters our country. After bearing down everything before it in its impetuous and rapid course, it at length becomes so shallow that women even can cross it on foot. But if you observe it in those places where it glides along gently, and is still, you will find that there its waters gradually deepen; it is respected by the nations, and it impedes the progress of armies."

Ever afterwards these people became the most faithful subjects of Bactra.

In the meantime, the King of Media had been

informed that Arsaces reigned in Bactra. The recollection of the affront he had received from him was revived in his mind. He resolved to declare war against him, and sought assistance from the King of Hyrcania.

"Join your forces to mine," said he in the letter which he wrote, "and let us prosecute our mutual revenge. Heaven destined the Queen of Bactra for your consort; one of my subjects tore her from your arms; come and regain her by force."

The King of Hyrcania returned this answer: "I should at this moment have been a slave among the Bactrians, had I not met with generous enemies. I return thanks to heaven which ordained that my reign should commence with misfortunes. Adversity is our mother; prosperity is only our step-mother. You would have me enter into a quarrel which is unworthy of a prince. Let us leave the King and Queen of Bactra to the enjoyment of their mutual happiness and love."

THE END.

www.ingramcontent.com/pod-product-compliance
Lightning Source LLC
Chambersburg PA
CBHW030849270326
41928CB00008B/1293